What God hath joined together...

By Harold Camping

**Printed and Published by
Family Stations, Inc.
290 Hegenberger Road
Oakland, CA 94621
1985, 1991**

Books by Harold Camping

Adam When?
Biblical Calendar of History
Feed My Sheep
The Fig Tree
The Final Tribulation
First Principles of Bible Study
Galatians Chapter One
Galatians Chapter Two
Galatians Chapter Three
The Glorious Garden of Eden
God's Magnificent Salvation Plan
The Gospel, God's Covenant of Grace
Let the Oceans Speak
Seventy Weeks of Daniel Nine
Sunday: The Sabbath
What God Hath Joined Together
What Is The True Gospel?
When Is The Rapture?

Other Bible guides by Harold Camping are available in paper and cassette form.

TABLE OF CONTENTS

INTRODUCTION

When we compare the church of today with the church of 50 years ago, we are astounded by the appearance of a most dreadful phenomenon. Fifty years ago divorce was almost unheard of. Oh yes, in some avant garde elements of our culture there were those who divorced; but in the church it was virtually never found.

But today divorce is as common as grass. Hardly a church exists wherein there are not people contemplating divorce. Not only are people in the pews divorcing, but deacons and elders and pastors are also divorcing. In short, the institution of marriage has become a shambles.

How did all this come about? Did the church of 50 years ago have a wrong understanding of the Bible's rules concerning marriage and divorce? Certainly the churches of our day that condone divorce are convinced that they have a biblical basis for their action. After all, doesn't the Bible teach in Matthew 19:9 that fornication is a cause for divorce? And doesn't I Corinthians 7:15 teach that the one that has been divorced is no longer bound to the divorced partner and, therefore, is free to remarry? Surely there is adequate biblical allowance for divorce and even remarriage after divorce.

Because this situation is so terrible and so all-pervasive, it would be well to examine the biblical principles concerning the subject.

It cannot be denied that something has dreadfully gone wrong. In the last 50 years the very foundation of marriage has been grievously shaken. Hardly a church exists without the problems of those who have been divorced, or of those who are contemplating divorce. The trauma to which the children of these unhappy marriages have been subjected is indescribable.

And along with the wreckage of families has come an overwhelming lusting after sexual pleasures and perversions. Indeed, it appears that Sodom must be moved down to second place as the capital of perversion and lust. What has happened to our world?

The magnitude and awfulness of this problem cannot be overemphasized. Marriage has everything to do with the family.

1

And the family is the foundation of society. It is the cornerstone of any and every nation. When the families are destroyed, the destruction of the nation is not far behind. Therefore it is imperative that we find a solution to this terrible plague that is sweeping over the earth.

In this study we will start and stand with the principle that the Bible is absolute truth. Only our understanding of it can be erroneous. As Christians we have an obligation to search the Word to discover all truth. And because God has much to say about the marriage relationship, we will examine most carefully all that the Bible has to say on this subject. In doing so we will rediscover the rules that God has given us for the purpose of protecting the marriage institution.

CHAPTER 1

BIBLICAL DIVORCE

We are embarking on a search for answers to a very serious and perplexing problem. The problem is to discover the truth about the binding character of the institution of marriage. In our day virtually every church and denomination has decided that under certain conditions a marriage can be broken. Indeed, not only can it be broken by divorce, but those divorced are permitted to remarry.

Such permissive rules are taught and preached as the Word of God. Solemnly pastors claim that they have the full authority of God Himself to encourage divorce under certain conditions and to call God to witness the joining together in marriage of those who have been divorced from their first spouse.

But what does the Bible say about this kind of activity? We must look carefully at all the Bible teaches to discover God's most holy will in this matter.

If we are ever going to understand the biblical teachings concerning marriage and divorce, we must start with an understanding of the ceremonial laws of the Bible. We must realize that it is in the ceremonial laws that God has first spoken concerning marriage and divorce.

As a matter of fact, it is the teaching of the ceremonial laws that has given many theologians of our day what they believe to be a biblical basis to permit divorce and remarriage. Without realizing it, in their misunderstanding of these laws, they have made a caricature of the ceremonial laws as they unknowingly have used them to justify today's divorces.

Therefore, we want to spend some time understanding the very nature of the ceremonial law itself and in particular its relationship to the world and the church of our day. And then we want to focus the spotlight of our study on the ceremonial laws that particularly relate to marriage and divorce.

WHAT ARE CEREMONIAL LAWS?

When Christ was on earth He spoke in parables and "without a parable spake He not unto them" (Mark 4:34). Sometimes Jesus told the people He was telling a parable. At other times He simply told a story and from its setting in the Bible we know it was a parable. For example, very frequently He would begin a story or a declaration with the words "the kingdom of heaven is like..." We know that when He used these particular introductory words He was teaching with a parable.

3

A parable is an earthly story with a heavenly meaning. That is, it is a story or illustration taken from the secular world, but its application relates to some aspect of salvation. It may teach some aspect of Christ's death or resurrection; it might relate to the faith that should be found in the life of the believer; it might emphasize the sending forth of the Gospel; or again, it might point to Judgment Day.

Because the nation of Israel was so intimately a part of the Gospel story, some of the parables were teaching about God's plans for them. For example, in Matthew 21:33-45, in the parable of the wicked husbandmen, Jesus is pointing to the fact that the kingdom of God would be taken away from national Israel and given to others.

In the Old Testament this same teaching method was used extensively. We can see this most clearly in the types and shadows God employed in the ceremonial laws outlining worship activities, and in the civil laws which governed much of the Israelites' civil pursuits.

These laws are called "ceremonial laws" by theologians because on the earthly, physical level they were to be rigorously obeyed by the nation of Israel. But once Christ hung on the cross, the physical aspect of these laws was no longer to be obeyed. Now only the heavenly meaning inherent within these laws is to continue. At the time Christ hung on the cross the great curtain that separated the holy of holies from the holy place was torn apart from top to bottom by the finger of God. This signaled the end of the literal, physical keeping of the ceremonial laws. From that time forward the eyes of believers were to be focused only on the spiritual teachings set forth in the ceremonial laws as opposed to the literal, physical keeping of the ceremonial laws.

The fact is, when the New Testament church met together to decide which of these ceremonial laws were to be obeyed by the Gentiles who were being saved, they concluded in Acts 15:28-29:

For it seemed good to the Holy Ghost, and to us, to lay upon you no greater burden than these necessary things;

That ye abstain from meats offered to idols, and from blood, and from things strangled, and from fornication: from which if ye keep yourselves, ye shall do well. Fare ye well.

By this statement we can see that the observing of ceremonial laws had come to an end.

The ceremonial laws ran the whole gamut from blood sacrifices and burnt offerings to such things as the dimensions and characteristics of the temple building, as well as to such things as laws concerning the planting of fields or weaving of cloth.

These laws were to be obeyed by Israel literally, as earthly experiences. But as they engaged in the earthly event they were to realize that the earthly event was only a shadow or type of some aspect of God's salvation. In Colossians 2:16-17 God emphasizes this principle as He declares:

Let no man therefore judge you in meat, or in drink, or in respect of an holyday, or of the new moon, or of the sabbath days:

Which are a shadow of things to come; but the body is of Christ.

Included within the ceremonial laws were laws concerning marriage. Three of these were especially noteworthy.

We shall look at each of these three laws very carefully. In doing so we will begin to understand the terrible dilemma the church of today has gotten itself into in this matter of divorce and remarriage after divorce.

BELIEVERS ARE NOT TO BE UNEQUALLY YOKED WITH UNBELIEVERS

The first of these three laws is found in Deuteronomy 7:2-4. This law was given to national Israel at the time they were first coming into the land of Canaan. The law declares:

And when the Lord thy God shall deliver them before thee; thou shalt smite them, and utterly destroy them; thou shalt make no covenant with them, nor shew mercy unto them:

Neither shalt thou make marriages with them; thy daughter thou shalt not give unto his son, nor his daughter shalt thou take unto thy son.

For they will turn away thy son from following me, that they may serve other gods: so will the anger of the Lord be kindled against you, and destroy thee suddenly.

The first part of this commandment points to the spiritual principle of the eventual judgment of the unsaved by the believers. This will occur at Judgment Day when the believers will act as the jury, judging those who must be sent to hell for their sins (I Corinthians 6:2; Revelation 2:26,27). The earthly

5

application of this commandment is that they were to destroy the nations of the land of Canaan.

The second part of the commandment points to the spiritual principle that believers were not to be unequally yoked with unbelievers. The nation of Israel typifies the body of believers in Christ. The heathen nations surrounding Israel typify the world with all of its enticements and temptations. Even as the men of the nation of Israel were not to marry heathen wives, so believers are not to become attached or "married" to the world.

As a further development of this law, God declares in Isaiah 52:11:

Depart ye, depart ye, go ye out from thence, touch no unclean thing; go ye out of the midst of her; be ye clean, that bear the vessels of the Lord.

In this exhortation the Israelites were effectively told that they were to divorce themselves from that which was unclean. In its literal, earthly application it meant that if (in violation of Deuteronomy 7:2-4) they had married heathen wives, they were to divorce them. The truth of this can be seen dramatically in the book of Ezra.

The last two chapters of Ezra reveal a most sad and traumatic experience faced by Israel. Under the leadership of men like Nehemiah and Ezra a number of Israelites had returned to Jerusalem. In Jerusalem the discovery was made that quite a number of the men had married heathen wives and had even borne children. We read in Ezra 9:2-4:

For they have taken of their daughters for themselves, and for their sons: so that the holy seed have mingled themselves with the people of those lands: yea, the hand of the princes and rulers hath been chief in this trespass.

And when I heard this thing, I rent my garment and my mantle, and plucked off the hair of my head and of my beard, and sat down astonied.

Then were assembled unto me every one that trembled at the words of the God of Israel, because of the transgression of those that had been carried away; and I sat astonied until the evening sacrifice.

In answer to this serious charge of violation of the commandment of Deuteronomy 7:2-4, the leaders of Israel made a very important and difficult decision. They decided that these men must be divorced from their heathen wives. We read in

Ezra 10:2-3:

And Shechaniah the son of Jehiel, one of the sons of Elam, answered and said unto Ezra, We have trespassed against our God, and have taken strange wives of the people of the land: yet now there is hope in Israel concerning this thing.

Now therefore let us make a covenant with our God to put away all the wives, and such as are born of them, according to the counsel of my lord, and of those that tremble at the commandment of our God; and let it be done according to the law.

The decision was to let it be done according to the law. In Isaiah 52:11 God's law decreed that those who had become involved with the unclean thing were to depart from that which was unclean. In the practical sense it was saying that if an Israelite married a heathen wife, he was to divorce that wife. This was precisely the way Ezra and the other leaders understood that law, for we read in Ezra 10:10-12 of their decision concerning this matter.

And Ezra the priest stood up, and said unto them, Ye have transgressed, and have taken strange wives, to increase the trespass of Israel.

Now therefore make confession unto the Lord God of your fathers, and do his pleasure: and separate yourselves from the people of the land, and from the strange wives.

Then all the congregation answered and said with a loud voice, As thou hast said, so must we do.

That we have not misunderstood the disposition of this problem can be seen further on, in Ezra 10:16-17.

And the children of the captivity did so. And Ezra the priest, with certain chief of the fathers, after the house of their fathers, and all of them by their names, were separated, and sat down in the first day of the tenth month to examine the matter.

And they made an end with all the men that had taken strange wives by the first day of the first month.

Combining the commands of Deuteronomy 7:2-4 and Isaiah 52:11 with the last two chapters of Ezra, we see that the earthly application of this first ceremonial law concerning marriage is that there was to be biblical divorce. If a man violated the law

7

of Deuteronomy 7:2-4 by marrying a heathen wife, the law of Isaiah 52:11 decreed that he was to correct that sinful situation by divorcing that wife.

The spiritual or heavenly meaning introduced by these laws continues today. In II Corinthians 6:14-17 God declared:

Be ye not unequally yoked together with unbelievers: for what fellowship hath righteousness with unrighteousness? and what communion hath light with darkness?

And what concord hath Christ with Belial? or what part hath he that believeth with an infidel?

And what agreement hath the temple of God with idols? for ye are the temple of the living God; as God hath said, I will dwell in them, and walk in them; and I will be their God, and they shall be my people.

Wherefore come out from among them, and be ye separate, saith the Lord, and touch not the unclean thing; and I will receive you,

By this law God is emphasizing that believers are not to be unequally yoked to anything that is of the kingdom of Satan. This can be someone we are planning to marry, or it can be any situation in which we become so entangled with the world that it is like being married to the world.

If we find this condition existing in our lives, we are to separate ourselves from it. We are to turn away from this unclean condition. This turning away from the world is what God was typifying by the biblical divorce presented in the last two chapters of Ezra.

MUST I DIVORCE MY UNSAVED SPOUSE?

Of course, our next question is fairly shouting at us by now. Since the men of Israel were to divorce heathen wives to whom they had become married, what about a mixed marriage of today wherein the believer is married to an unbeliever? Is the believer to divorce the unsaved spouse? In order to answer these questions, let's quickly review what we've learned so far.

The earthly story of the Old Testament was that some of the men of Israel were marrying women of other nations. Such marriages were to be ended by divorce. In the New Testament when God says "Israel" He means the body of believers. So, even as the Old Testament men of Israel were not to marry heathen women, the New Testament men of Israel, the true

8

believers, are not to marry unsaved wives. Does that mean then that God intends for a believer to divorce his unsaved wife?

God answers this question very carefully in I Corinthians 7:12-13.

But to the rest speak I, not the Lord: If any brother hath a wife that believeth not, and she be pleased to dwell with him, let him not put her away.

And the woman which hath an husband that believeth not, and if he be pleased to dwell with her, let her not leave him.

God further answers this question in 1 Peter 3:1 where He speaks of the wife who is married to the unsaved husband. There we read:

Likewise, ye wives, be in subjection to your own husbands; that, if any obey not the word, they also may without the word be won by the conversation of the wives;

In these verses God is indicating that there is not to be divorce in the case of this kind of marriage. We thus see that the earthly application of the ceremonial laws of Deuteronomy 7:2-4 and Isaiah 52:11 no longer is to be observed. No longer do these laws provide a valid basis for divorce.

But the heavenly meaning of these laws continues today. Anyone who is so involved in or attached to the world to the extent that he seems married to it is to turn away from it. He is to separate himself from this unholy alliance.

Thus we have seen that until Christ went to the cross a biblically sanctioned divorce was required when a man had violated Deuteronomy 7:2-4 by marrying certain heathen women. But the earthly aspect of this law came to an end when Christ died, as indicated by New Testament verses such as I Corinthians 7:12-13, II Corinthians 6:14-17, and I Peter 3:1.

But Deuteronomy 7:2-4 and Isaiah 52:11 are not the only ceremonial laws that speak to the question of marriage and divorce. In our next chapter we will look at another ceremonial law that focuses on the sanctity of marriage.

CHAPTER 2

ADULTERY CALLS FOR THE DEATH PENALTY

In the first chapter of this study we found that there was a time when, under certain conditions, divorce was sanctioned by the Bible. But we also learned that the earthly aspect of that divorce is no longer applicable. Insofar as marriage is concerned, the divorce that was sanctioned by the ceremonial laws we have thus far examined, is no longer applicable to us today.

But now we will look at a second ceremonial law that relates to marriage. It is found in Deuteronomy 22:22 where God declares:

If a man be found lying with a woman married to an husband, then they shall both of them die, both the man that lay with the woman, and the woman: so shalt thou put away evil from Israel.

This law did not deal with the prohibition of certain marriages as did the law of Deuteronomy 7:2-4. Rather, it demanded the death penalty for a man and woman who were discovered in an adulterous relationship. This dramatic judgment on those who commit adultery was the literal, earthly application of this command.

But what is the heavenly meaning? What is the Gospel application of this command?

The answer to these questions is found in the New Testament. There we discover that this command is pointing us to a very awesome spiritual marriage. This marriage is revealed in Romans 7:1-4. There we read:

Know ye not, brethren, (for I speak to them that know the law,) how that the law hath dominion over a man as long as he liveth?

For the woman which hath an husband is bound by the law to her husband so long as he liveth; but if the husband be dead, she is loosed from the law of her husband.

So then if, while her husband liveth, she be married to another man, she shall be called an adulteress: but if her husband be dead, she is free from that law; so that she is no adulteress, though she be married to another man.

Wherefore, my brethren, ye also are become dead to the law by the body of Christ; that ye should be married to another, even to him who is raised from the dead, that we should bring forth fruit unto God.

In this significant passage God teaches us that in a spiritual sense every individual in the human race is automatically married to the law of God. This marriage is not the result of man's desire. Rather, it is a marriage in which God has joined two parties together into an indissolvable union. These two parties are the human being on the one hand, and the law of God on the other hand.

Because God has joined these two together, no man can break this union. No matter how we might wish we were free from our spiritual marriage to the law of God, we cannot be freed from it.

Unfortunately, it is a marriage between a perfect husband and a very imperfect wife. The husband is the law of God, which is absolutely blameless. The wife, however, is the human being, and she is altogether adulterous. We know that the law of God is the husband because Romans 7:1 declares that the law has dominion over the man. Within any marriage relationship, it is God's plan that the husband is the head of the wife and that the wife is to be submissive to the husband.

Therefore, within this spiritual marriage, we humans are to submit obediently to the law of God, which is our spiritual husband. But each and every time we commit a sin we are engaging in spiritual adultery. We are not being faithful to our spiritual husband, the law of God.

The law of God, as the husband, cannot divorce the adulterous wife because what God has joined together cannot be put asunder by man. God takes this principle so seriously that even a perfect husband, the law of God, cannot become separated from the adulterous wife (each human) to which it is married.

That this spiritual adultery is recognized by God can be seen in the language of James 4:4.

Ye adulterers and adulteresses, know ye not that the friendship of the world is enmity with God? whosoever therefore will be a friend of the world is the enemy of God.

In this verse God is clearly speaking of the adulterous nature of mankind. Men are adulterers and women are adulteresses because they are living in spiritual fornication in relationship to the law of God to which they are spiritually married.

Jesus makes reference to this adulterous condition of the

human race by the language of Mark 8:38 where we read:

Whosoever therefore shall be ashamed of me and of my words in this adulterous and sinful generation; of him also shall the Son of man be ashamed, when he cometh in the glory of his Father with the holy angels.

The adulterous and sinful generation of which He speaks includes the existence of the whole human race throughout time.

The kingdom of Satan to which all of the unsaved of the world belong is described as the great whore in Revelation 17. This indictment of the world can be clearly understood when we realize that every unsaved person is married to the law of God. But because of man's sinfulness, he is living adulterously as a harlot. Each sinful act is an act of spiritual adultery.

However, even though the law of God, as the husband, cannot divorce that fornicating wife, the human race, there is a way that this terrible marriage can be brought to an end. Because of fornication, the wife deserves to die. Only if she dies can this unfortunate marriage be brought to an end.

Because the husband is absolutely just and holy, it (the law of God) will bring accusation against the adulterous wife, demanding her death. It is this death that was anticipated in the ceremonial law of Deuteronomy 22:22.

ONLY ETERNAL DAMNATION CAN BREAK THIS SPIRITUAL MARRIAGE

The earthly story required the physical stoning of both the adulterous wife and the individual with whom she had committed adultery. But the heavenly meaning of this terrible punishment is far more serious. This is because the death that is required by mankind's husband, the law of God, is the second death, which is eternal damnation. Only after we have spent an eternity in hell can the marriage between the law of God on the one hand, and each human being on the other, be ended.

When a man, a woman, or a child dies physically, does this death end the spiritual marriage of this person to the law of God? Unfortunately, it does not. For on the Last Day, when this individual is resurrected, this person's spiritual husband, the law of God, will stand there, accusing this person of spiritual fornication while living on this earth.

Even in hell the law of God is present, demanding the full penalty--an eternity in hell. Only if this person has spent an eternity in hell can he be freed from the dominion of the husband, the law of God. But because eternity is forever, there will never be an ending of this awesome relationship.

This, then, is the warning that God wants us to see in the ceremonial law of Deuteronomy 22:22.

The question must now be raised: Is the earthly aspect of this dreadful ceremonial law still to be observed in our day? The answer is that it (like all of the ceremonial laws) is no longer to be observed now that Christ has gone to the cross.

This is shown by Jesus' reaction to the woman taken in adultery, which is recorded in John 8:1-11. According to Deuteronomy 22:22, she should have been stoned. But Jesus, who is eternal God Himself, nullified that command by telling the woman to sin no more.

But the spiritual meaning of Deuteronomy 22:22 continues throughout time. This can be seen very clearly in the language of Romans 7:1-4. The recognition of this spiritual situation points us to our intense need of a Saviour. Later we will look at the wonderful truth that in Christ we can be freed from this dreadful marriage with the law of God.

ONLY DEATH CAN END THE HUMAN MARRIAGE

It must not escape our attention that, in discussing the spiritual application of this command, God has set it forth in the context of the human marriage relationship. The individual is bound forever to the husband, the law of God. Only death can break this union.

Likewise, the wife is bound to her husband as long as he lives. Only his death can free her from this marriage union.

The word "bound" that is used in Romans 7:2 is very important. We read there that the woman is "bound" to her husband as long as he lives. Only his death can free her from this marriage union.

The word "bound" is the Greek word "deo." It connotes being "shackled together." For example, in Mark 5:3 it is translated "bind" and in verse 4 as "bound." These verses describe its import and meaning as we read:

Who had his dwelling among the tombs; and no man could bind him, no, not with chains:

Because that he had been often bound with fetters and chains, and the chains had been plucked asunder by him, and the fetters broken in pieces: neither could any man tame him.

Again in Acts 12:6 we read of Peter in prison, "bound with two chains." This word "deo" is found many times in the Bible and is always used in the sense of someone who is tied or shackled.This is the word that God uses in describing the wife's relationship to her husband. This is seen in Romans 7:2 and also in I Corinthians 7:39 where we read:

The wife is bound by the law as long as her husband liveth; but if her husband be dead, she is at liberty to be married to whom she will; only in the Lord.

Again in I Corinthians 7:27 we read, "Art thou bound unto a wife ?..."

This binding or shackling of the wife to the husband can only be broken by the death of the husband as Romans 7:2-3 so plainly teaches. (As the law of God is the spiritual husband of each human being, forming a spiritual bond that cannot be broken, likewise the husband cannot divorce his wife even in the face of her continuous adultery.) She is bound to him as long as he lives.

How important it is that we see that, in no uncertain terms, God is teaching that there cannot be divorce for any reason whatsoever! As we go on in this study we will see this important principle more and more clearly.

HOW TO BECOME FREE FROM OUR MARRIAGE TO THE LAW OF GOD

Before we leave this second ceremonial law which demanded the death penalty for those caught in adultery, we should not miss the glorious teaching which shows us how we can end the spiritual application of this ceremonial law. That application points us to the traumatic fact that each of us, in our unsaved condition, is married forever to the law of God.

But in Romans 7:4 God gives us the way of escape:

Wherefore, my brethren, ye also are become dead to the law by the body of Christ; that ye should be married to another, even to him who is raised from the dead, that we should bring forth fruit unto God.

What does this mean: that we have "become dead to the law by the body of Christ"? We can understand this if we recall that the death required by our spiritual husband, the law of God, was eternal damnation. This is precisely the death Jesus endured when He took our sins upon Himself. In the atonement He was found guilty with our sins and God poured out His wrath upon Him as punishment for those sins. That punishment equaled the punishment we would have to endure if we had to spend an eternity in hell.

That is why Romans 7:4 indicates that Christ rose from the dead. This was the proof that the penalty demanded by the law of God had been entirely paid. Because Christ, our substitute, endured the equivalent of eternal damnation for each believer, each believer has become dead to their former husband, the law of God. Thus the law of God has no longer any dominion over him. He is dead to the law.

And he, as a new creature, as one who is born again, is free to become spiritually married to someone else. That someone else is Christ Himself. The believer becomes the eternal bride of Christ.

The spiritual marriage of the believer to the law of God has come to an end by the death of Christ because, as the believer's substitute, He has endured eternal damnation. Christ, therefore, is free to take the believer as His bride in an eternal marriage relationship. God has joined the believer to Christ in an eternal, indissolvable marriage relationship that no man can break asunder.

Since no death can ever occur to either Christ, the husband, or to the believer, the bride, there is no possible way that this beautiful marriage can ever come to an end. Even though the believer might engage in spiritual fornication (sin), Christ cannot divorce His bride.

Even as the law of God, the husband, could not divorce its fornicating wife (the unsaved person), so too, Jesus cannot divorce His bride, the person who has become saved, even when His bride commits spiritual fornication. Likewise, in the human marriage relationship, there cannot be divorce for fornication. What God has joined together cannot be put asunder. Only death can break this marriage.

Because the believer was given eternal life at the time of salvation, and because Christ rose from the dead to live forever, Christ can never end this blessed marriage union between Himself and the believer.

How marvelous! How wonderful! How magnificent is the grace of God!

Moreover, because the law of God is no longer the husband of the believer, it no longer has dominion over the believer. That is, never again can it threaten the believer with death. The eternal damnation Christ endured for each believer forever satisfies any penalty the believer might be subject to for spiritual fornication (for any sin he might commit).

15

This does not mean he is no longer related to the law of God. The law of God has now become his friend. It shows him how to enjoy to the highest possible degree his new relationship with his new husband, Christ Jesus Himself. But he is no longer shackled to the law of God the way a wife is to a husband. Therefore, the law can no longer threaten him with eternal damnation when he sins.

Wonderfully, even as God uses the marriage relationship between the law of God and mankind to help us understand human marriage between husband and wife, so too, God uses the wonderful marriage relationship between Christ and His bride to help us understand human marriage. Later in our study we will look at this more closely.

Thus far we have looked at two ceremonial laws which had to do with marriage. The first decreed that an Israelite was not to marry a woman of certain nations. If he did so, he was to divorce her. This law was pointing to the spiritual principle that we are not to be unequally yoked with the world. If we find we have become tied to the world, we are to break these ties. We are to depart from the unclean thing.

We discovered that the earthly application of this ceremonial law no longer is applicable. Since believers are found in every political nation, and national Israel no longer has preferred spiritual status (since the cross), this law no longer applies to marriages between individuals of different nationalities.

True, we can make an earthly application when we recognize that a believer is not to marry an unbeliever. This application is possible because the spiritual meaning continues throughout time. The marriage of a believer to an unbeliever is directly related to the spiritual meaning which decrees that there is not to be the yoking together of the kingdom of Satan and the kingdom of Christ.

But even in this special application, the Bible very carefully instructs us in the New Testament that there is not to be divorce even if a marriage does come to exist between a believer and an unbeliever.

The second ceremonial law we looked at was Deuteronomy 22:22. There we discovered that the earthly story insisted that a man was to have his wife stoned to death if she were found committing adultery. But this earthly application was set aside when Christ told the woman taken in adultery to "go, and sin no more."

On the other hand, the spiritual meaning of this ceremonial law continues forever. It points to the marriage between the human race and the law of God. The law of God, as the husband, rules over each unsaved individual, the wife. But no matter how often the wife engages in the spiritual adultery of rebellion against the law of God, there can be no divorce. Only eternal damnation satisfies the death penalty required because of mankind's spiritual fornication.

Thus far we have not found the slightest suggestion that, following the cross, there can be divorce for any reason whatsoever. On the contrary, we have found that even as we humans are bound to the law of God until we have completely experienced the second death, eternal damnation, so too, the wife is bound to her husband as long as they both shall live.

In the next chapter we will look at a third ceremonial law that actually has been used as the basis for much of the divorce that is taking place today.

CHAPTER 3

GOD'S MARRIAGE TO ISRAEL

Patiently we are carefully searching the Bible to find what it has to say about the institution of marriage. We are particularly seeking to know if under any circumstances a divorce may occur.

So far we have examined two sets of laws found in the Bible that relate directly to the questions we are studying. And thus far, we have found no statement that condones divorce for any reason whatsoever.

But now we shall look at a third ceremonial law that relates to marriage and divorce. It was introduced into the Bible because there existed a second spiritual marriage, entirely different from the marriage of the law of God to the human race. It was the marriage wherein God took as His wife a nation, ancient national Israel. Israel, as a corporate, external body, was the representation of the kingdom of God on earth during the historical period from Abraham to Jesus.

This marriage relationship was established by God because national Israel as a whole typified and foreshadowed the spiritual Israel of God which was to become the eternal bride of Christ.

We know this spiritual marriage between God and national Israel existed because of God's complaint recorded in Jeremiah 3:14 concerning the spiritual fornication practiced by His wife:

Turn, O backsliding children, saith the Lord; for I am married unto you:...

He was not married to them as individuals; as individuals they were spiritually married to the law of God. Rather, He was married to them as a corporate entity.

But God faced a real problem. At no time in national Israel's history were they faithful. Repeatedly they lusted after other gods. What was God to do with His fornicating wife?

According to God's eternal law, death is required for the adulterous wife. But God could not utterly destroy Israel as a nation, for it was out of national Israel that Christ was to come. Moreover, national Israel was to be the seedbed from which the whole New Testament church would spring forth.

Furthermore, God's plan was to use national Israel as an example of His patience and mercy. Remember, in the parable of Luke 13 the fig tree that repeatedly had not borne fruit was to be cut down. But then it was to be given one more opportunity. If there still was no fruit, it was to be cut down.

So today we see national Israel as a viable nation amongst

the nations of the world. Only if it ceases to bear spiritual fruit will it be destroyed.

For all these reasons, and possibly others, God chose not to have his spiritual wife, national Israel, killed. And yet it was God's plan to break His spiritual marriage with national Israel. Once Christ went to the cross, God had purposed to end forever any spiritual relationship He had ever had with Israel as a nation. nation.

To accomplish this goal, God introduced another law into the body of ceremonial laws. In order to divorce Israel God had to introduce a law that would permit divorce. God, as the giver and maker of the law, may introduce any law He desires. But whatever law He sets forth, God in His perfect righteousness obligates Himself to obey.

And so in Deuteronomy 24:1-4 God placed into the Word of God a law that permitted divorce for fornication. There we read:

When a man hath taken a wife, and married her, and it come to pass that she find no favour in his eyes, because he hath found some uncleanness in her: then let him write her a bill of divorcement, and give it in her hand, and send her out of his house.

And when she is departed out of his house, she may go and be another man's wife.

And if the latter husband hate her, and write her a bill of divorcement, and giveth it in her hand, and sendeth her out of his house; or if the latter husband die, which took her to be his wife;

Her former husband, which sent her away, may not take her again to be his wife, after that she is defiled; for that is abomination before the Lord; and thou shalt not cause the land to sin, which the Lord thy God giveth thee for an inheritance.

This law permitted a husband to divorce his wife in whom he had found some matter of uncleanness. (Later we will go into detail to show that this related to fornication.) The inclusion of this law permitted God to divorce national Israel. We are told this in Isaiah 50:1.

Thus saith the Lord, Where is the bill of your mother's divorcement, whom I have put away? or which of my creditors is it to whom I have sold you? Behold, for your iniquities have ye sold yourselves, and for your transgressions is your mother put away.

Likewise, in Jeremiah 3:8 we read:

And I saw, when for all the causes whereby backsliding Israel committed adultery I had put her away, and given her a bill of divorce; yet her treacherous sister Judah feared not, but went and played the harlot also.

Further on, in verse 20 of Jeremiah 3, God continues revealing the sinful nature of the wife He had married.

Surely as a wife treacherously departeth from her husband, so have ye dealt treacherously with me, O house of Israel, saith the Lord.

So we have seen that within the ceremonial law God introduced two dominant laws concerning adultery within a marriage. These two laws were quite different from each other. In the case of Deuteronomy 22:22 both a man and a woman engaging in the act of adultery were to be put to death. In the case of Deuteronomy 24:1-4, only the wife could be divorced for fornication. No language is employed here or anywhere else in the Bible that even suggests that a wife could ever divorce an adulterous husband.

Because these laws were a part of the ceremonial laws, the citizens of the nation of Israel were to obey them. If a husband found his wife in an open act of adultery, he was to have her stoned to death along with the man with whom she was caught. If there were some act of obvious fornication, but the wife was not actually caught in the act of adultery, the husband still had the right to divorce her.

This ceremonial law of Deuteromony 24:1-4 had an earthly, physical application and a spiritual, or heavenly application. As we have seen, the earthly application permitted the husband to divorce his wife if it appeared she had engaged in fornication. The heavenly application was intended to make it possible for God to divorce national Israel because of its continuing spiritual fornication.

Jesus made several references to this law in the New Testament. He did so to show that this law was rescinded with His coming as the Christ, as well as to show that Israel had grossly misapplied this law. Remarkably, it is still grossly misapplied by the church as a biblical basis for divorce. We will look into this as we continue our study.

ISRAEL'S MISUSE OF DEUTERONOMY 24

The language of Deuteronomy 24:1-4 was sufficiently unclear

so that the men of national Israel used it as a basis for divorcing their wives for any reason whatsoever. Let us see why this is so, because this will help us understand Matthew 5:32, a verse some people use to justify divorce for fornication.

The key words of Deuteronomy 24:1 are "some uncleanness." For "some uncleanness" found in a wife the husband had biblical cause for divorce. What exactly was this sin?

The Hebrew word "dabar," which is translated as "some" in the phrase "some uncleanness," normally means "word" or "matter." Out of about 2400 usages in the Bible, it is translated in at least 1000 verses "speak" or "talk" or something similar. In other verses it is translated "word" at least 770 times. Thus, "word" or "talk" are the dominant meanings of the word "dabar."

Less often, but with considerable frequency, "dabar" is translated as "act" (52 times), "matter" (63 times) and "thing" (215 times). Thus, we can safely say that in Deuteronomy 24:1 "dabar" should be translated as "act," "matter," "thing," or "word."

The Hebrew word which is translated as "uncleanness" in this same phrase is "ervah." It is a word that is found 54 times in the King James Bible. In more than 50 of these places it is translated "nakedness." When we examine the places where it is translated "nakedness" we find that it usually relates to gross sexual impurity. For example, in Leviticus 18 and Leviticus 20 where God is setting forth commands prohibiting incest, God employs the word "nakedness" ("ervah") at least 30 times.

Thus, the word "ervah" takes on the meaning "fornication." The fact is, in Leviticus 18:8 God warns, "The nakedness (ervah) of thy father's wife shalt thou not uncover." A commentary on this warning is found in I Corinthians 5:1 where we read:

It is reported commonly that there is fornication among you, and such fornication as is not so much as named among the Gentiles, that one should have his father's wife.

In this verse God uses the word "fornication" in connection with sexual impurity between a man and his father's wife. But in Leviticus 18:8 God speaks of this kind of sexual impurity as uncovering the nakedness. Therefore, we can see that "nakedness" or "uncleanness" is synonymous with "fornication."

Bringing these facts together, we can know that in Deuteronomy 24:1 God is teaching that if a man found a "word" or a "matter" of fornication in his wife, he could write a bill of divorcement and divorce her.

True, certain acts of fornication were punishable by death. But if the particular act or word of fornication did not require

21

the death of the fornicating wife, the husband had the right to divorce her.

But there was another understanding of the meaning of "ervah" that was possible. And it was this understanding that opened the door for the Israelite husband to divorce his wife under almost any circumstance.

DIVORCE FOR ANY CAUSE

In Deuteronomy 23:12-14 God used the identical phrase, "ervah dabar," which is used as the key phrase of Deuteronomy 24:1. "Ervah dabar" did not refer to fornication; rather, it referred to ceremonial uncleanness. Verses 12-14 inform us:

Thou shalt have a place also without the camp, whither thou shalt go forth abroad:

And thou shalt have a paddle upon thy weapon; and it shall be, when thou wilt ease thyself abroad, thou shalt dig therewith, and shalt turn back and cover that which cometh from thee:

For the Lord thy God walketh in the midst of thy camp, to deliver thee, and to give up thine enemies before thee; therefore shall thy camp be holy: that he see no unclean thing in thee, and turn away from thee.

The phrase "unclean thing" near the end of this quotation is "ervah dabar." But what was this "unclean thing"? In this context it was nothing more than the discharge from a person's body when he or she felt the "call of nature." When a person felt the urge, he was to go outside the camp, dig a hole to receive his body's discharge, and then he was to cover it so that the surface of the ground would be clean.

Actually, any discharge from the body made a person unclean. According to the ceremonial laws of Leviticus 15, any running issue, any kind of discharge from the body, made a person unclean. A woman menstruating was unclean. Someone experiencing diarrhea that spotted his garments was unclean.

Therefore, the use of "ervah dabar" in Deuteronomy 23:14 gave the men of Israel tremendous leverage in their marriages. All one had to do was to spot menstrual blood on his wife's garments; or any other discharge that touched her or her garments would serve the hardhearted husband's purpose. In the intimacy of marriage the opportunities to see "some uncleanness" in one's wife were numerous.

Thus the men could divorce their wives quite easily. The wife had no security whatsoever. Even though she may have never been guilty of fornication, the husband could still find plenty of "biblical" reason to divorce her if this was his desire.

JESUS SETS THE MATTER STRAIGHT

Significantly, Jesus took serious issue with this understanding of Deuteronomy 24:1-4. Jesus clarified the law by showing that these verses of Deuteronomy 24 had in view only fornication as a ground for divorce. We see this when we read Matthew 5:31-32. These verses declare:

It hath been said, Whosoever shall put away his wife, let him give her a writing of divorcement:

But I say unto you, That whosoever shall put away his wife, saving for the cause of fornication, causeth her to commit adultery: and whosoever shall marry her that is divorced committeth adultery.

The language of verse 31 relates back to Deuteronomy 24:1-4. This is the only passage of the Old Testament that relates in a clear way to the statement of Jesus found in Matthew 5:31.

But Jesus pointed out that ancient Israel had widened the application of cause for divorce far beyond the scope intended by Deuteronomy 24:1, where the cause had to be a specific word or matter of fornication. Most likely, by applying the words of Deuteronomy 23:12-14, they had decided that they could divorce their wives for any reason. That is why Matthew 5:31 states that all that was required for divorce at that time was the writing of divorcement. Jesus, therefore, made a point of restating Deuteronomy 24:1-4 in verse 32.

We will see that Jesus is accomplishing three things by this restatement. First of all, He is underscoring the Jews' total disregard for the sanctity of marriage. He is getting ready to show that the cause for divorce was to have been something quite adulterous.

Secondly, He is revealing the awful sinfulness of divorce in that it causes the divorced wife to commit adultery even though she, by her own action, might be innocent of adultery.

Thirdly, He restates the language of Deuteronomy 24:2-4 to show that the wife who was divorced should not remarry.

Let us look at Matthew 5:32 very carefully to discover these three things that Christ is emphasizing.

DEUTERONOMY 24 ALLOWS DIVORCE ONLY FOR FORNICATION

The first phrase we must understand in verse 32 is, "saving for the cause of fornication." Let us examine that phrase. We will see that it relates very closely to Deuteronomy 24:1.

The word "saving" is the Greek word "parektos." It is used in only two other places in the Bible. In Acts 26:29 it is translated "except":

And Paul said, I would to God, that not only thou, but also all that hear me this day, were both almost, and altogether such as I am, except these bonds.

In this verse "parektos" carries the meaning "without" -- "without these bonds."

The other place this word is found is in II Corinthians 11:28 where "parektos" is translated "without."

Beside those things that are without, that which cometh upon me daily, the care of all the churches.

Here we see that the biblical meaning of "parektos" is "without."

Returning to Matthew 5:32, we discover that the English phrase "for the cause" is the Greek word "logos." But "logos" is normally translated "word." It is translated as "word" more than 200 times in the Bible. It is also translated in a few instances as "matter" or "thing." Thus "logos" can mean either "word" or "matter" or "thing." And so we find that it actually is the Greek equivalent of the Hebrew word "dabar" used in Deuteronomy 24:1.

The word "fornication" used in Matthew 5:32 is the Greek word "porneias" which is always translated "fornication."
Therefore, we learn that the phrase "saving for the cause of fornication" can be accurately translated "without a word or matter of fornication." This is surprisingly close to the literal rendering of the Hebrew "ervah dabar" of Deuteronomy 24:1. Remember, the usual translation of "dabar" was "word" or "talk" or "matter;" and the usual translation of "ervah" was "nakedness" in the context of fornication.

Thus, we see evidence that Jesus was focusing in on Deuteronomy 24:1 by the specific language He used in Matthew 5:32. He was teaching that the "uncleanness" of Deuteronomy 24:1 was not meant to be understood as some ceremonial uncleanness such as menstrual blood or a diarrhea discharge. Rather, it was meant to present fornication as the only cause for which a man could divorce his wife. Deuteronomy 24:1-4 was never intended to give a man an excuse to divorce his wife for any cause.

DIVORCE CAUSES AN INNOCENT SPOUSE TO BE ADULTEROUS

As we continue to examine verse 32, we discover that Christ has introduced an additional principle to be kept in mind in the matter of marriage and divorce.

The next phrase in verse 32 is: "causeth her to commit adultery." How are we to understand this?

Let's begin by reading verse 32 without the phrase "saving for the cause of fornication." It now reads "whosoever shall put away his wife... causeth her to commit adultery." In this statement Jesus has introduced a very serious matter. While it is altogether wrong for a divorce to occur, should it occur, such a divorce causes the wife to commit adultery. Does this merely mean that the divorced wife becomes prone to adultery because, if she should marry someone else, that marriage would be adulterous as Romans 7:2-3 teaches?

No. There is no evidence that Jesus is teaching this. He is simply saying that if a man divorces his wife, regardless of how holy or pure she might be in herself, she has been forced by divorce itself to commit adultery. That is, the very act of the divorce caused her marriage to become adulterated and in that sense she has been caused to commit adultery. Jesus is underscoring how terrible the sin of divorce is. Not only does the husband who desires the divorce sin, but he also causes his wife to sin, even though she does not want the divorce.

This becomes understandable when we remember that those who have married have become fused by God into one flesh, a divine union which no man can break apart. Remember, we saw earlier in Romans 7:1-4 that the wife is bound to her husband as long as she lives. Therefore, if a man breaks apart that which God has joined together, the union has been adulterated. Even though the wife may be perfectly innocent in the divorce, she has been forced to commit adultery because the union with her husband has been adulterated. This is one of the important teachings of this verse. Jesus is emphasizing the fact that divorcing a wife for any reason was a dreadful sin.

However, if the wife had committed fornication before the divorce, then she herself committed adultery. Based on Deutero-onomy 24:1, the man had a right to divorce his wife in such a case. So, since she was adulterous before she was divorced, the husband's act of divorcing her was not the cause of her sinful state of adultery.

But Jesus is not calling attention to Deuteronomy 24:1 in order to indicate that this command is to continue in force throughout time. That is not the purpose of Jesus' reference to it. He is simply showing that while Deuteronomy 24:1 was in force, a man had to discover actual fornication in his wife. To put her away for any lesser cause was a violation of that command. And the Jews had grossly violated that command by perverting it into a command wherein they could divorce their wives for any cause.

But since that command was repealed (as we shall see when we study Mark 10 and Matthew 19), Jesus definitely is not teaching that fornication is a cause for divorce. Therefore, this verse is not dealing with the question of whether or not there is any cause for divorce. That question is not at issue. Rather, Jesus is emphasizing the seriousness of the sin of divorce. Divorce causes even the husband's spouse to commit adultery because the union between herself and her husband has become adulterated by this divorce.

THE WOMAN WHO IS DIVORCED BECOMES DEFILED IF SHE MARRIES AGAIN

The third point that Jesus makes involves a restatement and clarification of Deuteronomy 24:2–4 which reads:

And when she is departed out of his house, she may go and be another man's wife.

And if the latter husband hate her, and write her a bill of divorcement, and giveth it in her hand, and sendeth her out of his house; or if the latter husband die, which took her to be his wife;

Her former husband, which sent her away, may not take her again to be his wife, after that she is defiled; for that is abomination before the Lord: and thou shalt not cause the land to sin, which the Lord thy God giveth thee for an inheritance.

In our King James Bible it appears (by the use of the word "may" in the phrase "she may go ") to say that the fornicating wife who was divorced was free to remarry. However, in the original Hebrew the word "may" is not included. So the Bible is not teaching she may go and be another's. This can be seen by the language found in verse 4 where God indicates she will have become defiled if she remarries. Effectively, God is teaching that if the divorced wife goes and becomes another man's wife, she will be defiled so that she can never return to her first husband.

This principle is reiterated and expanded in the last phrase of Matthew 5:32 where Jesus declares that "whosoever shall marry her that is divorced committeth adultery." Because the divorced wife who has remarried has become defiled as a result of this remarriage, it logically follows that the man who married her has entered into an adulterous marriage. Jesus is emphasizing the fact that such a man has indeed committed adultery.

But in Matthew 5:32 Jesus is further indicating that anyone who marries a divorced wife is committing adultery. That is, if a wife is divorced for any reason, the man who marries her commits adultery. We see, therefore, that even as Romans 7:2-3 taught that the woman who remarried while her first husband was still living became an adulteress, so too, the man who married such a woman has become an adulterer.

DEUTERONOMY 24:1 ALLOWED ONLY ONE HALF OF ISRAEL TO DIVORCE

Significantly, the law that permitted a man to divorce his wife for fornication only applied to half of Israel. Let us see why this was so.

As we have seen, Deuteronomy 24:1 was a law that only permitted the husband to divorce his wife. This was so because, in its ceremonial nature, it was pointing to the coming divorce of national Israel. But no provision of any kind was made for the wife to divorce the husband. This was because there was no aspect of God's salvation plan or of God's dealing with national Israel that included the possibility of national Israel divorcing God. Therefore, as national Israel obeyed that law, a wife could never divorce a fornicating husband. In her relationship to her husband she was under the universal law given from the beginning of creation that there was not to be divorce for any reason whatsoever.

Thus, we see that in the case of the law of God (the husband) being spiritually married to the individual (the wife) there never was a time when divorce for fornication or for any other reason was allowed. Also we have seen that in the nation of Israel the wife could never divorce the husband for his fornication. Only the husband could divorce the wife for fornication because that was part of the ceremonial law pointing to God's coming divorce of corporate, national Israel. This was to occur because of their many spiritual fornications. It would come about when God no longer planned for national Israel to serve as a type or figure of His salvation program.

In summary, we see that Deuteronomy 24:1-4 taught the following principles:

1. A husband could divorce his wife only if she were found guilty of fornication.
2. The wife, who was guilty of fornication and, as a result, was divorced, would become defiled if she married someone else. Thus she was to remain single.
3. No permission was given to the wife to divorce her husband for any reason whatsoever.

In Matthew 5:32 Jesus reiterated the basic principles of Deuteronomy 24:1-4 and expanded them to teach:

1. A husband who divorced his wife for any reason other than fornication caused her to commit adultery.
2. Any man who married a divorced woman committed adultery.

Now we must face the next question.

When we looked at Deuteronomy 7:2-4 and Deuteronomy 22:22 we saw that once Christ went to the cross the earthly, physical applications of the laws no longer were to be observed. Only the spiritual or heavenly meanings of these commands were to continue.

But what about Deuteronomy 24:1-4? What does the Bible teach concerning the continuation of this law? Insofar as the spiritual, heavenly meaning of these verses is concerned, we know that it came to an end when Jesus hung on the cross. When the veil of the temple was rent asunder, it signaled the finality of God's divorce from national Israel. Never again would He have any spiritual relationship with national Israel as a corporate body.

Therefore, in its spiritual dimension, Deuteronomy 24:1-4 has no application after the cross. Because it was written into Old Testament law in order that God might divorce national Israel for its spiritual fornication, we have reason to suspect that it (like other ceremonial laws) ceased to have any physical application after the crucifixion. It was at that time that God officially ended His special spiritual relationship with national Israel.

The Bible clearly shows that this law was rescinded by the Lord Jesus Christ in Mark 10:2-12. Let us look at these verses.

In Mark 10:2 we read of the Pharisees coming to Jesus with a question concerning divorce. This verse informs us:

And the Pharisees came to him, and asked him, Is it lawful for a man to put away his wife? tempting him.

Their question must relate to Deuteronomy 24:1-4 for it is the only Old Testament passage that speaks of the possibility of a man divorcing his wife. This can be seen in Jesus' answer in verses 3 and 4:

And he answered and said unto them, What did Moses command you?

And they said, Moses suffered to write a bill of divorcement, and to put her away.

These verses plainly show that Deuteronomy 24:1-4 is in view. It is clearly the passage that Jesus is addressing as He continues to teach. In verse 5 Jesus explains why this command had been inserted into Old Testament law:

And Jesus answered and said unto them, For the hardness of your heart he wrote you this precept.

Here He declares that it was because of the hardness of the hearts of ancient Israel that the law was given to allow divorce for fornication. Can we assume by this that God saw how adulterous the wives in the nation of Israel would be? Did He want to provide some relief to the husbands by setting forth a law that permitted them to divorce if their wives were involved in fornication? Or did He give the law because the husbands would be so unforgiving of their fornicating wives that, because of the hardness of their hearts, these unforgiving husbands were allowed to divorce their wives?

Neither of these possiblities make sense. God lays down laws that help us to live more holy before Him rather than to allow us to live sinfully.

It is only when we realize the truth as to why God inserted this law into the ceremonial laws of the Bible that this verse can be understood. The phrase "hardness of heart" relates to that which is rebellious. And rebellion against God is spiritual fornication. God gave this law so that He, as the husband of national Israel, could divorce His fornicating wife. It was because of the hardness of heart, or spiritual fornication of national Israel that this law was given. And so, once God had divorced national Israel, this law had no further purpose.

Therefore, we find in verses 6-9 of Mark 10 that Jesus very directly, very plainly rescinds this command by stating:

29

But from the beginning of the creation God made them male and female.

For this cause shall a man leave his father and mother, and cleave to his wife;

And they twain shall be one flesh: so then they are no more twain, but one flesh.

What therefore God hath joined together, let not man put asunder.

In this answer Jesus indicates that it was never God's intention for divorce to be permitted. True, temporarily, God did open a very narrow window permitting a man to divorce his fornicating wife. But this was only so that God could divorce fornicating national Israel.

In Jesus' answer in Mark 10:9 He restates God's intention for marriage with the words: **"What therefore** God hath joined together, let not man put asunder." In other words, there is not to be divorce for any reason whatsoever. Two people who have been joined together in marriage have been fused by God into one flesh. And that which has been bound together by God, no man is to try to break apart.

To underscore this truth Jesus added in Mark 10:11-12:

And he saith unto them, Whosoever shall put away his wife, and marry another, committeth adultery against her.

And if a woman shall put away her husband, and be married to another, she committeth adultery.

Deuteronomy 24:1-4 allowed only a husband to divorce a fornicating wife. A wife was given no right whatsoever to divorce a fornicating husband. But now that Jesus has rescinded the husband's right to divorce a fornicating wife, He emphasizes the impossibility of biblical divorce from both directions—that of the husband divorcing the wife, and that of the wife divorcing the husband.

We see, therefore, that Jesus has clearly re-established the principle laid down from the beginning of time that there is not to be divorce. He is emphasizing what the Bible continues to declare in later verses.

Moreover, in Mark 10:11-12 God is underscoring another vital principle. It is the law that a divorced man or woman cannot become remarried. According to verse 11, if a man remarries, he commits adultery against his first wife. Why is this so?

Remember, we learned in Romans 7:1-4 that the wife is bound to her husband as long as they both live. Therefore, even though a divorce may have seemingly broken the marriage relationship, from God's vantage point the man and wife are still bound to each other. Therefore, if the man takes another wife while his first wife is still living, he is committing adultery. He is adulterating the lifelong union God has made between this man and his first wife.

Likewise, verse 12 emphasizes that the wife may not marry someone else after divorce. Even though she is legally divorced, in God's sight she is still bound to her first husband. Therefore, she commits adultery if she marries another while her first husband is still living.

Again, when we looked at Romans 7:1-4 we saw how God clearly teaches that the wife is bound to her husband as long as he lives. Remember, this statement was in the context of a wife living in constant fornication against her husband.

The principle of this binding relationship of the wife to the husband is repeated in I Corinthians 7:39.

The wife is bound by the law as long as her husband liveth; but if her husband be dead, she is at liberty to be married to whom she will; only in the Lord.

Moreover, in I Corinthians 7:10 we are instucted, "Let not the wife depart from (that is, divorce) her husband."

Likewise, in I Corinthians 7:11 God adds, "...and let not the husband put away his wife." All of the Bible's teachings are consistent and in agreement. There is not to be divorce for any reason whatsoever.

Significantly, in Luke 16:17 Jesus made reference to the eternal nature of the law of God as He declared:

And it is easier for heaven and earth to pass, than one tittle of the law to fail.

Having indicated the perpetual nature of the law of God, Jesus immediately addresses the question of a man divorcing his wife. He exhorts in Luke 16:18:

Whosoever putteth away his wife, and marrieth another, committeth adultery: and whosoever marrieth her that is put away from her husband committeth adultery.

In this statement we find a repetition of the same exact truth we have already learned from Mark 10:2-12, Romans 7:1-4, and

I Corinthians 7. There is not to be divorce! No exceptions are to be made!

We also find in Luke 16:18 the truth of Mark 10:11 repeated. God is again declaring a man is not to marry another after being divorced. Here in Luke we also find the last phrase of Matthew 5:32 re-emphasized. God is again teaching that anyone who marries a divorced woman commits adultery.

At this point, it is very clear that God does not countenance divorce for any reason whatsoever. In order to divorce national Israel (whom God had corporately married), He had temporarily put a law on the books allowing a husband to divorce his wife for fornication. But when Jesus came on the scene, He very deliberately and very clearly rescinded that special law.

We have further learned that there is not to be remarriage while a former spouse still lives. This truth also may be seen very clearly.

But you may ask, doesn't Matthew 19:9 teach that there still can be divorce for fornication? To answer this fair question, we will examine that verse in detail in the next chapter.

CHAPTER 4

MATTHEW 19:9

As we get more deeply involved with the biblical teachings on divorce, we want to look carefully at the one verse that has been abused most consistently in man's efforts to find a biblical basis for divorce. Because this verse immediately relates to Deuteronomy 24:1-4, which we studied at length in our last chapter, we are now prepared to understand Matthew 19:9.

This verse has the appearance of allowing divorce for fornication. It reads:

And I say unto you, Whosoever shall put away his wife, except it be for fornication, and shall marry another, committeth adultery: and whoso marrieth her which is put away doth commit adultery.

Many theologians read this verse and quickly conclude that it is teaching there can be no divorce except in the one case of fornication. Surely this verse appears to teach that fornication is cause for divorce.

But we have already seen in our study that there is no biblical cause for divorce. Neither fornication, nor any other sin on the part of either the husband or the wife provides any reason whatsoever for divorce.

Therefore, we can be sure that this one verse, Matthew 19:9, cannot allow divorce for fornication, or for any other reason. If we concluded otherwise, we would have before us a major contradiction.

But the Bible is one harmonious whole. While it may have statements within its text that appear contradictory, we can know that these are not actual contradictions. They only appear to be contradications while our understanding of the questionable passages remains incomplete. But when we have come to correct understanding, we will no longer find contradictions. This is so because the Bible is one harmonious whole.

But let us assume for a moment that we must base our whole understanding of divorce and remarriage on this one verse, Matthew 19:9. What would we learn?

Matthew 19:9 apparently teaches that a man may divorce his wife for fornication. But notice: there is no suggestion that the wife may divorce the husband for fornication. There is not even the slightest implication or indication that the wife can divorce the husband. In fact, nowhere in the Bible is there any statement that teaches that the wife can divorce the husband for any reason.

We also notice that the verse does not justify the husband for divorcing his wife for any reason except fornication. According to this verse, as it stands alone, the only possible cause for divorce is fornication.

Additionally, Matthew 19:8, which immediately precedes the verse we are studying, tells us that Moses allowed the husband to divorce his wife for the cause of fornication only because of the hardness of the husband's heart. The verse declares:

He saith unto them, Moses because of the hardness of your hearts suffered you to put away your wives: but from the beginning it was not so.

The term "hardness of heart" refers to someone who is unsaved, someone who is in rebellion against God.

Thus, if anyone insisted on understanding Matthew 19:9 without regard to any other teachings of the Bible, the most that he could see in this verse would be that a husband could divorce his wife only in the case of fornication. And such a divorce would be an indication of the husband's unsaved, rebellious spiritual condition. Therefore, even on the basis of Matthew 19:9, no true child of God would ever countenance the thought of divorce. Rather, he would realize that he is called upon to repeatedly forgive his wife for the sin of fornication just like any other sin.

When we consider what modern day theologians have done with this verse, we should become very skeptical of their conclusions, for when they have decided there can be divorce for the cause of fornication, they immediately conclude that, not only can the husband divorce the fornicating wife, but the wife also can divorce the fornicating husband. Yet neither this verse nor any other in the whole Bible allows a wife to divorce her husband. Thus when we hear such teachings, we should suspect that gross violation has been done to a true understanding of this verse.

To the question, "Does the Bible teach that fornication is a ground for divorce?" the answer is emphatically "No!" We have just seen that in Deuteronomy 24:1, God, as part of the temporary ceremonial law, had made fornication a cause for a man to put away his wife. Then we saw, as we looked at Mark 10, that through Christ that command was rescinded. Now we shall see that right in the context of Matthew 19:9, as Jesus makes reference to Deuteronomy 24:1, He is indicating the same teaching we discovered in Mark 10:2-12. That teaching was that Deuteronomy 24:1 was rescinded.

Let us see how this develops in Matthew 19. Again, we read in Matthew 19:8:

He saith unto them, Moses because of the hardness of your hearts suffered you to put away your wives: but from the beginning it was not so.

Here Jesus is emphasizing two important truths. First, this command was inserted into the law book primarily to give God a way to divorce national Israel because of their spiritual rebellion, their hardness of heart. Secondly, He is indicating that this was not God's eternal plan for human marriage -- "from the beginning it was not so." And as we discover from other passages that God's divorce of national Israel was finalized at the cross, we come to see that this law no longer applies. So by the language of verse 8 we see that He was effectively rescinding this law.

That Jesus is bringing to an end the Deuteronomy 24:1 basis for divorce for fornication is in total agreement with the statement of Matthew 19:8. It is also in complete harmony with the other passages we have looked at which emphatically prohibit divorce for fornication or for any other reason.

Since Jesus has just emphasized in Matthew 19:8 that a man was no longer to put away his wife for fornication, it doesn't make any sense at all that our Lord would reintroduce in the very next verse the command He has just rescinded.

NO DIVORCE FOR ANY REASON WHATSOEVER

We know, therefore, that we have to re-read Matthew 19:9 to attempt to discover what Jesus was actually saying in this verse. Certainly He was not teaching that fornication was a cause for divorce.

A correct understanding of Matthew 19:9 is forthcoming if we go back to the opening sentence of the paragraph in which Matthew 19:9 is found. In verse 3 of that chapter we read:

The Pharisees also came unto him, tempting him, and saying unto him, Is it lawful for a man to put away his wife for every cause?

The question the Pharisees are asking is whether a man can put away his wife for every cause. Jesus answered them in verses 4-6 by indicating there is not to be divorce for any reason whatsoever: "What therefore God hath joined together, let not man put asunder."

Then in verse 7 the Pharisees asked about Deuteronomy 24:1, which permitted divorce for fornication. Jesus answered their question in verse 8, indicating that Deuteronomy 24:1 was rescinded. It could no longer apply.

In verse 9 Jesus returned to the Pharisees' original question: "Can a man put away his wife for every cause?" In verse 8 He had indicated that fornication was no longer to be a cause for divorce. So in verse 9 He covers every possible reason other than fornication, indicating that any other reason was also an invalid cause for divorce. Effectively He is saying in verse 9, "whosoever puts away his wife for any reason 'in addition to' or 'other than' or 'except' for fornication (which we have just seen in verse 8 to be an invalid cause for divorce) and marries another commits adultery."

In other words, the word "except" (the Greek "ei me") takes on the sense or meaning of "in addition to" or "other than" in this context. This meaning of "ei me" is fairly common in the Bible. For example, in Matthew 19:17 Jesus said: "...there is none good but (ei me) one, that is, God:...." This verse could be read: "there is none good 'in addition to' or 'other than' one, that is, God."

Likewise, in Mark 8:14 we read:

Now the disciples had forgotten to take bread, neither had they in the ship with them more than one loaf.

The phrase "more than" is also "ei me." Here, too, we could translate: "neither had they in the ship with them 'in addition to' or 'other than' one loaf."

Many other examples could be given, but these two should suffice to show that Jesus, in Matthew 19:9, is simply covering all other possible causes for divorce "except," "other than," or "in addition to" fornication. He has already eliminated the cause of fornication in verse 8.

Jesus has thus twice answered the question posed by the Pharisees in verse 3 concerning divorce for every cause. He has first answered it in verses 4-6 by indicating there is not to be divorce for any reason. Then in verses 7 and 8 He specifically teaches that fornication cannot be a cause for divorce. And in verse 9 He applies this teaching to all other causes for divorce, except the cause of fornication, which He had just covered in verse 8. Thus, the conclusion stands twice over. There is not to be divorce for any cause whatsoever!!

The removal of fornication as a cause for divorce so shocked the disciples that they said to Jesus in verse 10:

His disciples say unto him, If the case of the man be so with his wife, it is not good to marry.

They apparently could not envision a marriage wherein a husband had lost all right to divorce his wife. As we saw earlier in our study, Deuteronomy 24:1 had become a very convenient escape route for a man who no longer cared for his wife. Remember what this law declared: according to Israel's understanding of this command, all the husband had to discover was a word or matter of uncleanness. Any ceremonial uncleanness was sufficient to permit a husband to divorce his wife.

Thus, the disciples were astounded and dismayed that there could no longer be divorce. Their reaction to the statements Jesus made in Matthew 19:4-9 underscores the fact that Jesus had just rescinded the command of Deuteronomy 24:1.

Thus, we see that, even as the earthly application of the other ceremonial laws came to an end when Jesus came, so too, the application of this ceremonial law of a man divorcing his fornicating wife also ended with His coming. In fact, not only did the physical application of this law end, but the spiritual application ended as well.

The last half of Matthew 19:9 -- "and shall marry another, committeth adultery: and whoso marrieth her which is put away doth commit adultery" -- is almost an exact duplication of Luke 16:18. Remember, we saw that in this verse of Luke 16, as well as in Matthew 5:32 and Mark 10:11-12, God indicated that a man was not to marry another wife after divorce, and anyone who married the divorced wife committed adultery. Clearly the law stands today that as long as the divorced spouse lives, there is not to be remarriage after divorce.

Thus far, we have examined three different sets of ceremonial laws dealing with marriage and divorce. First we looked at Deuteronomy 7:2-4 and Isaiah 52:11 and saw that God prohibited an Israelite from intermarrying with people of certain nations. If they did so in violation of God's law, they were to separate from that which was unclean. In the physical, earthly aspect of this command they were to divorce their wives if they had married in violation of God's original command. We saw in I Corinthians 7:12-13 and I Peter 3:1 that the physical, earthly aspect of this command was rescinded when Christ came. However, the heavenly, spiritual meaning of this command continues throughout history. We are not to be unequally yoked with the world. If we find we are effectively in the embrace of the world, we are to turn away from it. Spiritually, we are to separate from the world so that we can serve God with our whole heart.

The second command we looked at was given in Deuteronomy 22:22 where God commands that a husband who finds his wife in the act of adultery is to have her stoned to death. The husband could not divorce her. He could only separate from his adulterous wife by having her executed.

We saw that the spiritual meaning of this command points to the spiritual marriage described in Romans 7:1-4. There God declares that every person is spiritually married to the law of God which is the husband. Because of our constant spiritual adultery against the law, we are to be executed. And the execution God has in view is eternal damnation. In this context God taught that even as a human cannot be divorced from the law of God because of spiritual adultery, a human marriage cannot be broken because of fornication. It can be broken only by death.

We discovered that the physical application of Deuteronomy 22:22, which called for the death of the adulterous wife, was rescinded. But the spiritual application continues today. Because of our spiritual adultery, our husband, the law of God, condemns us to eternal damnation.

Thirdly, we looked into the ceremonial law of Deuteronomy 24:1-4. This law decreed that if a man found even a word or act of fornication in his wife, he could divorce her. In the physical sense, as a man divorced his fornicating wife, he was being shown by God that likewise the nation of Israel, which corporately was married to God, would be divorced by God because of Israel's constant spiritual fornication.

Incidentally, we might remember that the Bible records that when Joseph, the stepfather of Jesus, thought Mary had committed fornication because she was with child, he, being a just man, sought how to put her away (Matthew 1:19). The fact that the Bible says he was a "just" man underscores the fact that God was absolutely holy and righteous when He divorced national Israel as a corporate body.

We might remember that God divorced them as a corporate body, not as individuals. God could not divorce them as individuals within the nation because He was not married to them on that level.

On the other hand, the law of God as the husband was married to them as individuals and in that relationship there could be no divorce. No matter how adulterous any man became, he remained under the law of God, even as the wife remains under the dominion of her husband.

Thus we see that God used national Israel to display various types and figures which were shadows of the spiritual reality which was to be fulfilled in Christ. Their corporate marriage to

38

God was to be a picture of the marriage of Christ to the eternal church. Even as God married Israel when it was a nothing, the believer becomes the bride of Christ when he is spiritually dead in his sins. Even as God lavished his love on his wife, national Israel, by showering them with physical and spiritual blessings, so He showers spiritual blessings on His eternal bride, the true believer in Christ.

But, as it was with all of the ceremonial shadows, the typology of God's marriage to national Israel was quite imperfect. The time would come when national Israel would no longer serve as a type -- the marriage of God to national Israel was to come to an end.

That is why God introduced the command given in Deuteronomy 24:1-2 as an integral part of the ceremonial law. This law anticipated Israel's spiritual fornication which allowed God to divorce them.

Once Christ went to the cross, national Israel's role of serving as a type or figure of God's salvation program came to an end. All ceremonial laws were completed in Christ, including Deuteronomy 24:1-2.

Thus, God's purpose for calling attention to Deuteronomy 24:1-2 in the New Testament is to emphasize that this temporary law no longer applies. Instead, the universal law given from the very beginning is the only law that stands: under no circumstance is there to be divorce.

It is in such passages as Romans 7:1-4 and Mark 10:2-10 that God shows us that that universal law still stands. Even while the ceremonial law was temporarily allowing a man to divorce his fornicating wife, God strictly limited that law to the nation of Israel.

As we go on in our study, we will look at a couple of verses found in I Corinthians 7 which frequently are used as a basis to justify divorce and remarriage. We will look at them in our next chapter.

CHAPTER 5

THE UNSAVED SPOUSE BREAKS THE MARRIAGE

Thus far in our study we have found no biblical basis whatsoever to justify divorce. In marriage God has joined two people together. No one is to put asunder that marriage. Moreover, should divorce occur, remarriage is not to be sought as long as both spouses still live.

But now we should examine a verse that is sometimes used as a biblical basis for remarriage after divorce. In I Corinthians 7:15 we read:

But if the unbelieving depart, let him depart. A brother or a sister is not under bondage in such cases: but God hath called us to peace.

We have been learning from Matthew 5, Matthew 19, and Mark 10 that the one who marries a divorced person commits adultery. But doesn't I Corinthians 7:15 teach that if the unbelieving spouse insists upon a divorce, the believing spouse is no longer bound in that marriage, and therefore is free to remarry?

We know from our previous studies that the conclusion that a divorced person can remarry is erroneous. So how are we to understand I Corinthians 7:15?

The key word that we need to understand is the word "under bondage." It is the Greek word "douloo" which means "to enslave." It is from the Greek word "doulos" which is translated "slave", "bondservant," or "servant" in the Bible. It is a word that is commonly used of a man's relationship to Christ. Paul was a servant (doulos) of Christ (Romans 1:1). We are servants of Christ (Colossians 4:12; II Timothy 2:24). On the other hand, we may be the slave of sin (II Peter 2:19).

But this word "doulos" or "douloo" is never used of the relationship that exists between husband and wife. Insofar as the Bible is concerned, the husband is never the slave of the wife; the wife is never the slave of the husband.

True, God does say in I Corinthians 7:27, "Art thou bound unto a wife?...." But this word "bound" is an entirely different word than "doulos" or "douloo." It is the Greek word "deo." It is a word that gives the sense of two things being bound or tied together. The prisoner is bound (Mark 6:17). The donkey was tied (Mark 11:2). The husband and wife are bound to each other (I Corinthians 7:27,39; Romans 7:2). But the idea of being a servant or a slave is not found in the word "deo."

But how do we explain the use of the word "douloo" in I Corinthians 7:15? It is a word that nowhere else in the Bible is identified with the husband-wife relationship. So how are we to understand its use in this verse? The answer can be seen if we properly understand the problem being addressed by this verse.

Let's look at a situation common to our day. The Christian wife knows there is not to be a divorce under any circumstance. But the unsaved husband insists on a divorce. He refuses to obey God's Word because he is unsaved. God's Word means little or nothing to him.

What, then, is his wife to do? Is she bitterly and relentlessly to fight her husband in order to prevent the divorce? God has an answer for this situation. She is called to peace. She is not to fight. In her bondage to Christ, earnestly desiring to do God's will, she is not to fight the divorce. She is not bound to Christ's written law to the point that she is to engage in such a fight.

If her husband insists upon divorcing her, she still cannot remarry as long as her husband is living. Remember Romans 7:2-3:

For the woman which hath an husband is bound by the law to her husband so long as he liveth; but if the husband be dead, she is loosed from the law of her husband.

So then if, while her husband liveth, she be married to another man, she shall be called an adulteress: but if her husband be dead, she is free from that law; so that she is no adulteress, though she be married to another man.

Do you recall that we learned from Matthew 5:32 and Matthew 19:9 that anyone marrying the divorced wife commits adultery?

Instead of marrying, she should remain unmarried or else be reconciled to her husband as I Corinthians 7:11 teaches.

But and if she depart, let her remain unmarried, or be reconciled to her husband: and let not the husband put away his wife.

We thus must realize that I Corinthians 7:15 is not intended to give aid or comfort to those seeking divorce. When carefully understood in the light of everything else the Bible teaches about marriage, this verse is found to be in perfect agreement with the · principle that there is not to be divorce for any reason.

41

ART THOU LOOSED FROM A WIFE?

As we continue our study, let's look at another passage that is sometimes made to serve as a rationale to permit divorce. In I Corinthians 7:27–28 we read:

Art thou bound unto a wife? seek not to be loosed. Art thou loosed from a wife? seek not a wife.

But and if thou marry, thou has not sinned; and if a virgin marry, she hath not sinned. Nevertheless such shall have trouble in the flesh: but I spare you.

When we try to understand the phrase "seek not to be loosed," it is very apparent and certainly biblical to understand this as a command not to seek divorce. That conclusion agrees with everything we have seen in the Bible concerning marriage.

But verses 27 and 28 go on to say, "Art thou loosed from a wife? seek not a wife. But and if thou marry, thou hast not sinned."

With this statement in mind, the argument is often presented that if the first word "loosed" in verse 27 refers to divorce, then the second word "loosed" must also refer to divorce. This interpretation makes this seem as if it is teaching that someone who is divorced can remarry.

But the conclusion, when tested by all the passages of the Bible that speak of divorce and remarriage, is shown to be wrong. Nowhere else in the Bible does God permit remarriage after divorce. In fact, in the verses we have examined we have seen that the man who marries after divorce commits adultery and the man who marries the divorced wife commits adultery.

Therefore, we should know that somehow we have arrived at an altogether wrong conclusion concerning the meaning of this verse. It does not fit with the rest of the Bible.

How then are we to understand this passage? Let us look more carefully at these verses.

First of all, we had assumed that the word "loosed" was referring only to divorce. Actually, there were two ways a husband could be loosed from a wife. She could have been divorced, or she could have died. Therefore, verse 27 is simply saying, "Art thou bound (Greek (deo.) Remember this word means (shackled to.) to a wife? seek not to desire to be loosed;" that is, don't desire that God would take her in death, which would be the biblical means of ending this marriage. And don't desire to be divorced from her. That would be the unbiblical way of attempting to end this marriage.

But if you are loosed from a wife, then what? Verse 28 declares you can remarry. Since there is clear evidence in the Bible that one can not remarry if they have been divorced, we can be sure that in this second usage of the word "loosed" God cannot have divorce in mind. If He did so, this verse would be contradicting everything else in the Bible concerning the subject of marriage and divorce.

The only possible meaning that can be in view in regards to this second usage of the word "loosed" is that the shackle that has bound the wife to the husband has been broken by her death. That conclusion is in total agreement with passages like Romans 7:1-4 where we learned that only death can break the union that exists between husband and wife.

As a matter of fact, even the first usage of the word "loosed" in I Corinthians 7:27 cannot refer to divorce. This is so because Romans 7:2 stipulates that only if her husband is dead is a wife loosed from the law of her husband. In other words, even if a husband divorces his wife, she is still bound to him insofar as God's law is concerned. Only death can loose her from her husband. Therefore, when God speaks of a man being loosed from his wife, He can be referring only to a loosing caused by the death of his wife.

Thus we learn that I Corinthians 7:27-28, like all of the other passages we have examined, gives no assent whatsoever to the idea of divorce or remarriage after divorce.

Now that we have concluded that there does not exist any possibility of divorce, let us look more closely at the marriage relationship and see how the husband and the wife are to live together as they are shackled together for the rest of their natural lives.

We will be asking these questions: Is marriage a contract? Is it a partnership between two people who stand on the same ground? How much does the Bible teach concerning the nature of marriage? We will examine these questions as we continue our study.

CHAPTER 6

LET NOT MAN PUT ASUNDER

We have thus far learned that marriage can be dissolved only by God Himself. He alone has the authority to terminate it by taking either one or both spouses in death. No other authority has the power to terminate a marriage, and death is the only valid means used by God to end a marriage.

In this chapter we will look more closely at the marriage union itself. We will ask: Is it just a partnership between two people who stand on the same ground? Is it merely a contract that is analogous to any other contract with which we might be familiar?

As we have been carefully examining all that the Bible teaches concerning marriage, we have begun to discover that marriage is not a contract; it is not a partnership. It is a union -- a union of such consequence that two people, as it were, have become fused into one being. The Bible uses the language: "they are no more twain, but one flesh" (Matthew 19:6).

The husband and wife have become fused together, or welded together, in such a way that God speaks of them as "one flesh." In fact, the wife is bound to her husband as long as he lives. As we saw when we studied Romans 7:1-4, even if the wife marries someone else, she is still bound to her first husband. It is a fusion, therefore, that men may try to break by divorce, but that in actuality only God can break. The man who divorces and marries another woman has, in God's sight, become married to two wives. This is true even if the law of the land recognizes only the latter wife, for God's law supersedes man's laws.

The intensity and reality of this fusion are further described in I Corinthians 7:3-5 where we read:

Let the husband render unto the wife due benevolence: and likewise also the wife unto the husband.

The wife hath not power of her own body, but the husband: and likewise also the husband hath not power of his own body, but the wife.

Defraud ye not one the other, except it be with consent for a time, that ye may give yourselves to fasting and prayer; and come together again, that Satan tempt you not for your incontinency.

In this statement God has established the principle that the two who are married are to live in the greatest possible intimacy. Their bodies belong to each other. Except for brief spiritual activity, they are not to deny their bodies from each other. No other physical relationship exists in the world like this relationship. They are to live as one body, because God has ordained that they are one flesh.

Moreover, God emphasizes that this union is not made by man but by God. Remember we read in Mark 10:9: "What therefore God hath joined together, let not man put asunder." Is this statement referring only to a Christian marriage under the authority of the church? If so, then all non-christian marriages would not be marriages. They would simply be a condition of two people living together in an adulterous relationship.

But the fact is, God is speaking of every marriage found in the human race. We can know that God has all marriages throughout history in every part of the world in view, for Mark 10:6-8 takes us all the way to our first parents who were created to be husband and wife. This indicates that God has in mind the whole human race. These verses tell us:

But from the beginning of the creation God made them male and female.

For this cause shall a man leave his father and mother, and cleave to his wife;

And they twain shall be one flesh: so then they are no more twain, but one flesh.

We know from these verses that whenever two people are joined in marriage and consummate that relationship in the marriage bed, it is a union made by God.

This is indeed a remarkable truth! It is hard to find any other physical human experience wherein we can say conclusively, "This is God's action."

Even the marriage that may have been consummated as an act of rebellion against God is still a marriage which God makes into an indissolvable union. But this does not make God guilty of sin, because God cannot sin. Rather, in accomplishing His divine purposes, God utilizes the sinful desires of man.

For example, God allowed the brothers of Joseph to commit the dastardly crime of selling their younger brother to be slave so that in turn Joseph, as Prime Minister of Egypt, would be able to later save them from starvation. Likewise, God can utilize a sinfully contracted marriage for His own purposes. And God informs us that once a marriage is consummated there has come into being a union by the action of God. Under God's edict, these two people who have become married to each other have become fused into one flesh. The moment two people become married, God informs us, the bond between them becomes more than just a human bond. It has become a bond in which God ordains that the two have become one flesh. God has welded or bound them into one body. No other human relationship is of this nature.

For that reason God speaks of the wife being bound to the husband (Romans 7:2; I Corinthians 7:39). And if the wife is bound to the husband, then it logically follows that the husband is bound to the wife. Earlier in our study, we saw that the word "bound," which God uses in these verses, means to be "tied to" or "shackled together." And remember that God declared that only He could break that union. He does this claiming one spouse in death. By God's edict, marriage has a distinction that sets it apart from every other human experience.

THE MARRIAGE UNION MAY NOT BE BROKEN BY MAN

As we saw earlier in this study, the fusion of the husband and wife is so complete that God warns in Mark 10:9:

What therefore God hath joined together, let not man put asunder.

This warning indicates that, since it is God who has fused the bodies of the husband and the wife into one flesh, no man is to separate that union. God reserves that right to Himself. He breaks the union by taking one of the spouses in death. But no man may break that union.

Actually counselors who encourage quarreling spouses to try a trial separation are in violation of God's Word. Divorce, which is so much in vogue in our day, is a terrible violation of God's edict concerning marriage. Rather than encouraging separation, the Bible insists that the bodies of those who are married belong to each other (cf. I Corinthians 7:3-5). No matter how badly the marriage is going, that principle is to be observed. Woe unto us when we take these matters into our own hands!

God again underscores the sacredness of the marriage union by declaring in Mark 10:11-12:

And he saith unto them, Whosoever shall put away his wife, and marry another, committeth adultery against her.

And if a woman shall put away her husband, and be married to another, she committeth adultery.

46

As we discovered earlier in this study, God further reinforces the certainty of this law that there is not to be divorce in Romans 7:2,3.

For the woman which hath an husband is bound by the law to her husband so long as he liveth; but if the husband be dead, she is loosed from the law of her husband.

So then if, while her husband liveth, she be married to another man, she shall be called an adulteress: but if her husband be dead, she is free from that law; so that she is no adulteress, though she be married to another man.

In Luke 16:18 Jesus restates the same principle by use of the words:

Whosoever putteth away his wife, and marrieth another, committeth adultery: and whosoever marrieth her that is put away from her husband committeth adultery.

Surely the Bible could not be any clearer! There is not to be separation! There is not to be divorce!

We might wonder why God has put such emphasis on the sanctity of marriage. God Himself has declared that He is the One who has joined these two people together; and no man is to break this union.

We can first of all see that God in His mercy has placed great protection around the family. These laws protect the husband and the father so that he is included in the family as long as any of the other family members are living. The wife is protected in the same way. Moreover, the same protection is afforded the children.

In our day, when divorce has become rampant in our land, we all know too well of wives who are trying to get along without husbands, husbands who have rejected their wives, and bewildered, broken children who hardly know who their parents are. Indeed, when the church first began to rewrite the rules of the Bible to permit divorce, it was the beginning of the end for families. The wind was sown, but the whirlwind is being reaped.

There is a staggering amount of evidence in the lives of broken families to indicate that the church committed drastic sin when it began to tamper with God's marriage laws. It's like the mythical Pandora's box, the lid of which could not be closed when sin began to pour forth. We have begun to see the reality of the magnification and terrible consequences of tampering with God's sacred laws. Indeed, it is with utmost peril that anyone dares to break apart what God Himself has welded together.

47

There is a second wonderful reason why God Himself enters into every marriage, claiming responsibility for the fusing of two people into one flesh. God uses the human marriage as a picture of Christ and the believers. Even as God fuses the husband and wife into one flesh, so God through the Lord Jesus Christ makes Himself one with the believers.

This unique oneness is spoken of in many different ways in the Bible. The believer is "in Christ Jesus" (Romans 8:1); Christ is in the believer (Romans 8:10); God the Holy Spirit dwells within the believer (Romans 8:11); and Hebrews 2:11 declares:

For both he that sanctifieth and they who are sanctified are all of one: for which cause he is not ashamed to call them brethren,

More specifically, the believers are called the bride of Christ (Revelation 21:2,9). And in the most beautiful language of Ephesians 5:28-32, God develops the human marriage as a type or figure of Christ's relationship to the believer. There we read:

So ought men to love their wives as their own bodies. He that loveth his wife loveth himself.

For no man ever yet hated his own flesh; but nourisheth and cherisheth it, even as the Lord the church:

For we are members of his body, of his flesh, and of his bones.

For this cause shall a man leave his father and mother, and shall be joined unto his wife, and they two shall be one flesh.

This is a great mystery: but I speak concerning Christ and the church.

In this passage God carefully declares that the joining of the husband to the wife as one flesh is pointing directly to Christ and the church.

Thus we see that God has placed His divine hand on the marriage union because He has made it a type or figure of the intimate and eternally binding relationship that exists between Christ and the true believers, His church.

Even as the husband and wife live together in the greatest intimacy, so Christ lives in a similar intimacy with the believer. And even as God has fused the husband and wife together into one flesh, so God has fused Christ and the believer together in such a way that God can use the same phrase, "one flesh," when speaking of this spiritual union.

Likewise, just as no one can break the human marriage union, so the marriage of Christ and the believer cannot be broken. It is an eternal union. What comfort we may have as we realize that once God has joined us as a believer to the Lord Jesus Christ, no man can break that union!

Death is the only way the physical union of husband and wife can be broken. But the believer in Christ has eternal life. That is, he can never die spiritually. And since Christ is eternal God, who died once at the cross and will never die again, there is no possibility of breaking the union between Christ and the believer. Neither the bride (the believer), nor the husband (Christ) can ever die. Therefore, no sinful action on the part of the believer can threaten his marriage with Christ. Even as in human marriage there cannot be divorce for fornication, the spiritual marriage between Christ and the believer cannot be broken by the spiritual fornication of the believer. What tremendous comfort and assurance we should receive from this glad truth!

Let us now look once again at the marriage relationship. What reservations or conditions may the husband place on his love and fidelity to his wife? And, what reservations can the wife place on her love and obedience to her husband? In our next chapter we will examine these questions.

CHAPTER 7

THE HUSBAND'S UNCONDITIONAL LOVE

We should now be fully impressed by the biblical evidence that shows us that a marriage can be terminated by God only as He takes one or both spouses in death. But now we want to examine the question: Even though a husband cannot divorce his wife for any reason whatsoever, is he to love her under all circumstances?

The Bible commands in Ephesians 5:25, "Husbands, love your wives." Does this command apply even when the wife does not love the husband? Does it apply when the wife indicates she hates her husband, when she may be on drugs, or is a drunkard, or is living in fornication? Surely God would not expect the husband to love this kind of a wife.

The fact is, however, that God's command to the husband to love his wife is unconditional. There are to be no reservations insofar as his love for his wife is concerned. No matter what she might be or become, he is to love her.

How do we know that this is so? First of all, we know this is so because the Bible offers no advice concerning conditions for a cessation of this love. True, Matthew 19:9 and Matthew 5:32 appear to indicate there can be divorce in the event of fornication. But earlier in our study, when we looked at these verses most carefully we discovered that in no way are they giving fornication as a cause for divorce. Likewise, I Corinthians 7:15 at first appears to teach there can be divorce in the case of desertion. But we learned as we looked at this verse most carefully that it is not teaching divorce at all.

Even in these verses that sometimes seem to suggest the possibility of divorce, there is no suggestion of a cessation of love. In fact, God teaches in Matthew 18:21-22 that forgiveness is to be normative in a Christian's life. We read in those verses:

Then came Peter to him, and said, Lord, how oft shall my brother sin against me, and I forgive him? till seven times?

Jesus saith unto him, I say not unto thee, Until seven times: but, Until seventy times seven.

If there is to be no end of forgiveness toward the one who has sinned against us, surely this principle of forgiveness should apply to the husband-wife relationship. Therefore, no matter what the wife does or says that displeases her husband, he is to forgive her. The principle, "Husbands, love your wives," still stands. Since a husband is never to cease forgiving and loving his wife, we can see even more clearly why God does not countenance divorce for any reason whatsoever.

Earlier, when we looked briefly at Ephesians 5, we saw that human marriage typifies the marriage union between Christ and the believer. Let us now develop that truth a bit further.

AS CHRIST LOVED THE CHURCH

As we look more carefully at Ephesians 5:25, we see a second dynamic reason why a husband's love for his wife is to be without reservation. This verse informs us:

Husbands, love your wives, even as Christ also loved the church, and gave himself for it;

In this important verse God is giving us an example of the kind of love the husband is to have for his wife: "even as Christ loved the church." What does this teach us? How did Christ love the church? Remember; the church that God has in view is the body of true believers in the Lord Jesus Christ.

How and when did Christ first love me as His child? How does He continue to love each of His believers after they become saved? Let us examine these questions a bit further.

What is the character of Christ's love towards those whom He plans to save? He loves them when they are still entirely rebellious against Him. He loves them without any conditions or reservations of any kind. He draws them to Himself when they are still in rebellion against Him. He inclines their hearts to love Him. He pays for their sins. He forgives every sin they will ever commit.

To accomplish this salvation Christ denied Himself entirely. He was stripped of the glory He had eternally with the Father. He humbled Himself to the lowest possible degree, becoming one with this sinful human race which arrogantly had rebelled against Almighty God. Even though Jesus Himself was without sin, He became laden with our sins. Worse than that, He bore the punishment demanded by God for those sins. That punishment was the worst that will ever be endured by anyone, for it was the equivalent of eternal damnation on behalf of everyone who would come to be His bride.

Indeed, God has given us an awesome example of the way husbands are to love their wives, as well as the kind of sacrifices they are to make as they seek the very best for their wives.

But what about after we are saved? Does Christ's relationship to His bride change? Again we stand amazed at the compassion, the patience, the forgiveness of Christ. No matter how often the true believer sins, Christ always forgives him. He promises He will never leave him nor forsake him. His love is a tender, everlasting love. Nothing His bride can say or do can separate her from Christ's love.

And this is the way the husband is to love his wife. No matter what she does or what she becomes, he is to love her; he is to cherish her as his wife. He is to patiently forgive, no matter how sinful or rebellious she might become toward him. And even as Christ, in His love for the church, wanted the very best for the church, so husbands are to always want the very best for their wives. Indeed, Christ paid an enormous price to free the believers from eternal damnation.

In his love for his wife, a husband will find that many times he has to deny himself. For the good of his family he may have to give up his cherished hobby. He may find that he cannot spend the time he would like to spend with his special friends. It may mean that he may have to reconsider his own personal thinking concerning the vocation he would like to follow or the place where he would like to live. Always he must have a loving concern for the feelings and needs of his wife and children.

As head of the house, he is not to consider himself to be the "the big boss." While he never loses sight of his responsibility as the head of the family, and that it is his wife's responsibility to submit to him, he nevertheless always tries to think of what is best for his wife and family. He lovingly guides his family. Always, his is the final authority under God; but he exercises that authority with great love, tenderness, and empathy for his family.

Under no circumstances is he to be resentful toward his wife. Whatever she is or does, he is to patiently continue to love her. He is never to think about others he could have married. He is never to look at other women and wish his wife could be like someone else. He is never to countenance the idea that he wishes he was married to someone else. The full focus of his attention and concern should be, first of all, toward his wife and family. No matter how difficult the situation may be, he is never to think of divorce. It is his business to love his wife regardless of what she is or does.

He is to accept without any reservation whatsoever the fact that his wife is to be an integral part of his life as long as she lives. Because God has fused her to him so that they are one flesh, he knows that he can never take any action that disregards his wife. His wife should be at least as important to him as anything else in his life. Only his love for his Savior should be greater than his love for his wife. And in his love for his Savior he knows he is to love and care for his wife the same way and to the same degree that he loves and cares for himself.

The greatest blessing a man should desire for his wife is, of course, eternal life. Therefore, a husband is not only to provide for the necessary physical needs of his wife; he is, above all, to provide for her spiritual needs. That is, he has the responsibility of providing a godly home. He has the responsiblity of leading his family in the fear and nurture of the Lord.

Moreover, Ephesians 5:28-29 declares:

So ought men to love their wives as their own bodies. He that loveth his wife loveth himself.

For no man ever yet hated his own flesh; but nourisheth and cherisheth it, even as the Lord the church:

The God-fearing husband has realized the highest possible good for himself. That good is salvation. Furthermore, he will do whatever is necessary to care for and satisfy the needs of his own body. This comes very naturally to him. But in these verses he is exhorted to love his wife as he loves his own body. If his body becomes ill, wounded, or otherwise troubled, he still loves it. Likewise, he is to love his wife the same way. No matter what moral, mental, or physical difficulties his wife may experience, he is to love her.

And because he is saved, he knows that finally his body, too, is to be changed into a glorious spiritual body. Just so, he is to desire the highest blessing -- a glorified spiritual body -- for his wife.

Moreover, he is to honor and respect his wife. We read in I Thessalonians 4:4:

That every one of you should know how to possess his vessel in sanctification and honour;

The vessel God has in view in this verse is the wife. The husband is to regard his wife as a holy vessel. She is not a convenient place to discharge his sexual lusts. In the marriage bed, as well as in all of his relationships with her, he is to treat her with honour and respect. To use a secular phrase, he is always to be a gentleman. In all things lawful he is to have a first concern for his wife.

Of course, no husband can of himself love his wife in the measure asked for by God. But by God's grace and in His strength, as the husband trusts more and more in Christ, these ideals become possible. Instead of ideals, they become living facts in the life of the husband.

As we ponder these truths, we begin to sense the awesome

responsiblity of the husband to love his wife -- to love her without condition or reservation -- to love her as long as she lives. With this mandate set before the husband, how could he ever think of divorce? The word "divorce" should not even be in his vocabulary. No wonder the old marriage forms declared:

I, John, take thee, Jane, to be my wedded wife, to have and to hold from this day forward, for better for worse, for richer for poorer, in sickness and in health, to love and to cherish, till death do us part according to God's holy ordinance; and thereto I give thee my troth.

CHAPTER 8

THE WIFE'S UNCONDITIONAL LOVE

We have seen most clearly that the husband is to love his wife without reservations of any kind. Regardless of her rebellion, her sinfulness, her unfaithfulness, or anything else, he is to love her as Christ loves the church. He is to faithfully forgive again and again.

But what about the wife's relationship to the husband? Because of the problem of unsaved husbands being married to Christian wives appears to be a far more serious and prevalent problem today than that of Christian husbands being married to unsaved wives, we will spend considerably more time with this question.

The Bible tells us in Ephesians 5:22, "Wives, submit yourselves unto your own husbands..." Is this submission to be without condition or reservation? Surely, if she respects him and he is a man worthy of her respect, she would be submissive to him. But what if he turns out to be a scoundrel, a drunkard, a philandering adulterer, or a wife beater? What then? Is she still to be submissive to him? Does she have to live like a doormat for him to walk all over? This is a very practical question in the light of the terrible way some husbands treat their wives.

The Bible speaks very directly and specifically to this question. There is no need to speculate or guess about what she is to do while married to such a husband.

First of all, Matthew 18:21-22 applies to her in the same way it applies to her husband. Remember; there the Bible teaches:

Then came Peter to him, and said, Lord, how oft shall my brother sin against me, and I forgive him? till seven times?

Jesus saith unto him, I say not unto thee, Until seven times: but, Until seventy times seven.

If she is a Christian, this passage leaves her no alternative but to forgive again and again as her husband sins against her.

A TYRANT OF A HUSBAND

God deals more specifically with this problem in I Peter 2 and 3. In I Peter 2:18-24 God deals with the matter of the servant who works for a cruel, ruthless, despotic master. There we read:

Servants, be subject to your masters with all fear; not only to the good and gentle, but also to the froward.

For this is thankworthy, if a man for conscience toward God endure grief, suffering wrongfully.

For what glory is it, if, when ye be buffeted for your faults, ye shall take it patiently? but if, when ye do well, and suffer for it, ye take it patiently, this is accceptable with God.

For even hereunto were ye called: because Christ also suffered for us, leaving us an example, that ye should follow his steps:

Who did no sin, neither was guile found in his mouth:

Who, when he was reviled, reviled not again; when he suffered, he threatened not; but committed himself to him that judgeth righteously:

Who his own self bare our sins in his own body on the tree, that we, being dead to sins, should live unto righteousness: by whose stripes ye were healed.

In these verses God indicates very clearly that it is our mission in life to bear patiently the injustices, the revilings, and the abuse of those who rule over us. We are not to revile in return. We are to realize that God has called us to walk in the footsteps of our Lord. We are to look to Him as our example. And the abuse He endured included His death on the cross.

In the opening verses of I Peter 3 God ties the admonishments of I Peter 2 to the wife who is married to an unsaved husband. The Bible exhorts in I Peter 3:1-5:

Likewise, ye wives, be in subjection to your own husbands; that, if any obey not the word, they also may without the word be won by the conversation of the wives;

While they behold your chaste conversation coupled with fear.

Whose adorning let it not be that outward adorning of plaiting the hair, and of wearing of gold, or of putting on of apparel;

But let it be the hidden man of the heart, in that which is not corruptible, even the ornament of a meek and quiet spirit, which is in the sight of God of great price.

For after this manner in the old time the holy women also, who trusted in God, adorned themselves, being in subjection unto their own husbands:

56

The important word "likewise" in verse 1 ties these verses of chapter 3 to the instruction which has just been given in chapter 2. Effectively, God is exhorting: "Even as the servant of a cruel master is to patiently endure abuse, so too, the wife who is married to a cruel husband is to patiently endure abuse." Note that verse 1 of chapter 3 is emphasizing that the husband in this case is one who does not obey the Word. That is, he is someone who is in rebellion against God. He, therefore, pays no attention to God's rules which declare that the husband is to love his wife and that he is to forgive her repeatedly.

The word "likewise" also implies that he, like the master of I Peter 2, may be unjust, cruel, and a tyrant in the home.

Human reason would conclude that if this is the condition in the home, the wife has every right to separate from her husband. No human should have to live under such unhappy, difficult conditions.

But God has a different answer. The word "divorce" is not to be a part of the wife's vocabulary. She must make it her business to love her husband as God commands. And because God always wants the very best for the human race, God's laws are the only trustworthy rules to follow. God declares she is to be quietly submissive to her difficult husband.

Two principles are being established in I Peter 3:1. The first is that she is not to nag, accuse, or preach to her husband. The second is that she is to be submissive to him. Let us look at each of these principles more closely.

The natural God-honoring inclination of the God-fearing wife of an unsaved husband is to desire his salvation. She earnestly desires his salvation, because she knows that apart from salvation her husband is headed for hell. He is under the wrath of God because of his sins.

Secondly, she desires his salvation because in the human sense she is embarrassed before her friends and relatives to be married to such a godless husband. Oh, how happy she would be if he would be a believer like the other husbands she sees in church every Sunday.

Thirdly, she desires his salvation because she knows that it would mean her trauma of being married to a difficult tyrant of a husband would have come to an end. She knows that then her husband would desire the very best for her as he showed his love to her. This would be the new situation, because a believing husband wants to obey God's command to love his wife as Christ loves the church.

Thus, there is much at stake as she prays for the salvation of her husband. And she knows that salvation comes by the Word of God and that she herself is commanded by God to be a witness. She seeks every possible occasion to share the Gospel with her husband. Certainly, she reasons, this activity on her part is in accord with the will of God.

WITHOUT A WORD

But God says, "No!" If her husband is to be saved, he is to be won without the Word. But why would God teach this apparently impossible program? Does God have one means by which He saves normal unbelievers a..d another program whereby He saves husbands? We know that can't be true. But why, then, this curious admonition that the wife is to be silent?

We can begin to understand this language if we see the special condition that prevails in the husband-wife relationship. When we bring the Gospel to others, normally these people know very little about our personal lives. Therefore, all that the unbeliever usually sees is the Gospel itself.

But, if a minister preaches from the pulpit, "Thus saith the Lord," while it is a well known fact that he is living in sin, his preaching will have little power. Those who hear him speak only look upon him as a hypocrite. In such a case the elders ought to be dealing with this pastor, even seeking to remove him from his role of pastor, if necessary.

Likewise, if we know someone who seems to be an ardent witness of the Gospel, and yet does not live the Gospel, we will not take him seriously. He, too, will be looked upon as a hypocrite.

In the husband-wife relationship this problem becomes especially enormous. A church body can know something about the thinking and actions of their pastor, but not everything. An unsaved person may know something about the life of the one witnessing to him, but not everything.

But a husband knows more about his wife's thinking and actions than anyone else could possibly know. He has lived, and may still be living with her, in the most intimate relationship. He is with her when she goes to bed and all through the night. He is with her in the morning before she's had her first cup of coffee to settle her nerves. He is with her when she is tense, when she is tired, when she is depressed, and when she is angry.

Because of the intimacy of their marriage, he knows by the way she walks, by the way she looks at him, by the way she greets him when he comes home from work, by the way she puts food on the table and by countless other mannerisms, whether she is thinking lovingly or resentfully towards him.

Therefore, even though she claims to be such a fine Christian, insisting on going to church, and insisting that her husband

58

repent from his sins and trust Christ as Savior, her husband knows very well that often she lives quite differently from the way she preaches to him. So he is likely to be convinced that whatever Christianity his wife has, he doesn't want it. He senses hypocrisy in his wife. If this is what a Christian is, he does not want to be a Christian.

He may not know that the Bible declares that his saved wife should have an earnest desire to forgive him again and again. He may not know that the Bible declares that a saved wife is not to nurse resentful feelings against her husband. He may not know that the Bible exhorts believers to walk very patiently. He may not know that the Bible states that the wife's body belongs to the husband and, therefore, in the bedroom she is to give herself willingly, warmly, and lovingly to him. He may not know that the Bible emphasizes that the wife is to submit to her husband in all things lawful. He may not know that his wife is to accept him as her husband without reservations of any kind. He may not know many or any of these principles.

But he does sense that his wife's actions do not measure up to her words. She is telling her husband to go to church, to obey God, to be a better husband. But as he thinks about times his wife has reacted to situations just like any other unbeliever, he becomes convinced she is altogether hypocritical. And his defences against the Gospel become increased if he senses any negative feelings from his wife toward him. As he thinks about his wife's attitude toward him, her resentment toward him, her coldness in the intimacy of the bedroom, her mannerisms and words that suggest very strongly that she would be happier without him as a husband, he knows one thing very well. If this is what being saved is all about, he wants no part of it at all.

True, if the husband is doing negative things against the wife, her congregation will look upon her as a loving child of God who unfortunately is married to a beast of a husband. When she is with her friends, when she talks to the pastor, when she sits in church, she appears to be a lovely, devoted wife who dearly loves to do the will of God.

But none of these dear people in the congregation can know her as her husband does. They cannot know how cold and resisting she may be in the marriage bed. They cannot know about the resentment she shows toward her husband. They have no way of knowing this wife like her husband knows her. Neither can they know the intense frustration of a husband living with a wife who in the most intimate relationship of the marriage does not practice what she preaches.

Therefore in I Peter 3:1 God admonishes the wife to reach her husband's heart by silent submission. Let her very quietly obey God's rules without preaching to her husband. Because of the tremendous intimacy that exists between husband and wife, her actions will speak far louder than any words.

Incidently, the same admonition should apply to the saved husband who is married to an unsaved wife. If the saved husband's intimate lifestyle does not clearly show the fragrance of Christ, his wife will look upon him as a hypocrite; she will not wish to emulate him. Truly, in the intimacy of marriage, the old adage "actions speak louder than words" certainly applies.

Returning to the saved wife's relationship to her unsaved husband, let the wife make sure that she accepts her husband without reservation. She should reject any thoughts of wishing she was not married to her husband. She realizes it is a dreadful sin to wish she had married someone else, or to wish that her husband could be like someone else. She knows full well that God has joined her to her husband and he is the only man she is to love and desire as a husband.

GOD GIVES THE RULES

The believing wife earnestly seeks to practice the principles set forth in Philippians 4:8. This verse outlines the kind of thinking that should be going on in the life of the believer. There she reads:

Finally, brethren, whatsoever things are true, whatsoever things are honest, whatsoever things are just, whatsoever things are pure, whatsoever things are lovely, whatsoever things are of good report; if there be any virtue, and if there be any praise, think on these things.

She, therefore, asks God's forgiveness when she thinks resentfully of her husband. When her husband sins against her, no matter how often this has been true in her marriage, she gladly forgives him. No matter how her husband treats her, she tries to convey to him that she is glad she is married to him.

She can do this honestly because she realizes that God has fused them into one flesh. She realizes that since they are married, her life will remain intimately involved with her husband until God Himself takes one of them in death.

The impact of this kind of godly behavior on an unsaved husband is bound to be enormous. Even though he is unsaved, he knows that he is wrong when he mistreats his wife. And as he sees her continuing faithfulness to him, her quiet submission, her continuing forgiveness, he will slowly realize that his wife is very special. By God's grace he should begin to relate his wife's beautiful conduct to Christianity. And by God's grace God may use this awareness to begin to open his spiritual eyes. This is the essence of the teaching of this helpful and hopeful verse of I Peter 3:1.

However, this kind of patient, submissive conduct toward a tyrant of a husband may not be understood by friends and relatives. Because they may not understand God's laws, they may tempt this dear wife by accusing her of being a "doormat" or a "patsy" or whatever.

But because she is truly saved, she has within her an earnest desire to do the will of God. This continuing desire will be an integral part of her life, as I John 2:3-6 teaches.

And hereby we do know that we know him, if we keep his commandments.

He that saith, I know him, and keepeth not his commandments, is a liar, and the truth is not in him.

But whoso keepeth his word, in him verily is the love of God perfected: hereby know we that we are in him.

He that saith he abideth in him ought himself also so to walk, even as he walked.

The only time she is to disobey her husband is if he asks her to break God's laws. If he asks her to lie, steal, or engage in sexual activity with someone other than himself, she, of course, must disobey. Such disobedience may bring her husband's wrath on her. However, if she has been the God-fearing, quietly submissive wife God asks her to be, without question her husband's wrath will be greatly reduced from what it might have been had she not been faithfully obeying God's rules by her quiet submission.

THE WIFE'S SECRET WEAPON

One area of special concern may arise if her husband forbids her to go to church or engage in other spiritual activities. After all, God commands in Hebrews 10:25:

Not forsaking the assembling of ourselves together, as the manner of some is; but exhorting one another: and so much the more, as ye see the day approaching.

Shouldn't she, therefore, disobey her husband when he makes such an unreasonable request? Or, if he forbids her to teach the children the ways of Christ, doesn't God command in Ephesians 6 that children are to be brought up in the fear and nurture of the Lord? What should she do when her husband makes these kinds of demands?

A direct answer to these questions cannot be given until other factors are considered. This is so because actions in the wife's life sometimes bring about such distressing confrontations about church. One big factor concerns the fact that the wife has a weapon she can use against her husband for which he has no defense whatsoever. The confrontation concerning church may be his way of getting even with his wife for using this weapon against him.

What is this powerful weapon? It is a weapon that the wife may wield without any deliberate malice towards her husband, or she may even employ it consciously to put him in his place. It is not a weapon of physical strength. Ordinarily the wife is physically much weaker than her husband. It is not the weapon of an agile mind whereby she can outwit her husband in some way. Rather, it is the weapon of a lack of submission in the intimacy of the bedroom. Because of its serious nature, we should look at this more closely.

Suppose a husband is very thoughtless toward his wife. He may even be quite cruel toward her. She can show her resentment toward him by reacting with cutting remarks, by giving him the silent treatment, or similar treatment accorded to her by her husband. But, if she is truly saved, she realizes this kind of conduct is altogether rebellious against God.

Nevertheless, all of these types of conduct the husband can deal with. He can be even more threatening. He can become more vicious in his verbal attacks on his wife. He might even resort to beating her. Since everyone who starts a fight wants to win the fight, the husband, too, wants to win.

While nothing is resolved by such exchanges between a husband and wife, and the marriage is grievously threatened by them, nevertheless, the husband feels equal to such challenges, insults, and treatment from his wife. Because he normally is physically the stronger of the two, he can feel that in some way he has won.

But in the bedroom the wife has a weapon that can drive the husband wild. Even though he may be a cruel, thoughtless husband, he knows that the greatest joy he has ever experienced is when his wife lovingly gave herself to him in the intimacy of the bedroom. It is an intimacy that is far more important to him than he realizes. For God has fused him into one flesh with his wife. Therefore, anything that destroys the joy of that intimacy is a blow to the very center of his manhood.

The problem is, however, that in order to experience the joy and wonder of the marriage bed, his wife needs to have warm and loving thoughts toward her husband. But when fighting has been going on, the wife feels defeated before this tyrant of a husband and she finds herself incapable of reacting with loving submission to his advances in the marriage bed. She may even try to avoid the marriage bed altogether; or if it looks like it can't be avoided, she may be cold and unresponsive to his advances.

Soon she learns that nothing bewilders, hurts, and frustrates her husband more than her lack of loving submission to his advances. And because she can not win the shouting match, she can not win the test of physical strength, she may opt for a miserable pleasure in the fact that in the bedroom she can be the winner.

This is so because nothing her husband does of a negative nature can force her to change. He can threaten, bully, or beat her, but all this only makes his wife even more unresponsive to his advances and as a result deepens his own frustrations and anger.

Without realizing it, the wife is laying the groundwork for another day of estrangement, quarreling, silent treatment, or cruelty which the husband uses to try to get even for the tremendous battle he just lost in the bedroom.

True, the husband and wife are not rationally thinking about what is happening. They are only reacting with the intuition of the sinful tendencies that dwell within them.

It is at such a point that the husband may try to strike back to even the score. What can he take from his wife that she loves the most? Aha! She is a Christian and is always making a big point of going to church, or listening to Family Radio, or reading the children Bible stories. These activities seem to bring the greatest pleasure to his wife. He, therefore, knows how he can really hurt her. He will forbid her from going to church. He will forbid her from listening to Family Radio, and so on.

All that the members of the congregation can see, is an unregenerate tyrant of a husband who is in rebellion against God. They, of course, haven't the slightest idea of what is going on in the marriage bed.

Meanwhile, the wife can go about appearing to be a martyr and receiving the sympathies of her friends. She may not even realize that her conduct in the marriage bed (as legitimate and logical as it may seem to her) is reprehensible to God. She is violating God's rule that she is to be in quiet submission to her husband. She is violating God's rule that she is to continuously forgive her husband. She is violating God's rule that her body belongs to her husband.

In fact, this weapon of unresponsiveness in the marriage bed should never be used. It will drive the husband into the arms of another woman quicker than anything else. It will serve to destroy the marriage more quickly than anything else. This is so because it is tampering with God's design of making the two one flesh.

On the other hand, let's consider the wife who loves the Lord and is living by God's rules. Her unsaved husband may begin to wonder, "How can I be married to such a wonderful, forgiving, thoughtful woman?" He may become increasingly embarrassed by his own thoughtlessness and cruelty. So when she asks if she can go to church on Sunday, he has no reason to deny her. He doesn't need to get even with her.

One could logically ask at this point, "Are you saying that all the problems of marriage begin in the marriage bed?" The answer is that they may not necessarily begin there. But it is there that they can be greatly advanced. And it is also there they can to a very high degree become solved.

True, the idea of becoming one flesh with one's spouse embraces much more than just the marriage bed. But it is there that it is the most obvious that the two become one flesh. That is why it is one of the most sensitive areas in the marriage relationship.

Before we leave the matter of the Christian wife's relationship to her unsaved husband, we should emphasize one other problem that is common to this situation. At the time this lady married her husband she was quite sure she loved him. But after the honeymoon was over, and after living with him in the confines and intimacy of the marriage relationship, she found that he had many qualities she did not like at all. He made unwise decisions. He was self-centered. He squandered the money that should have been used to buy groceries. He was lazy. He couldn't hold a job. She found that all her dreams about a pretty white house with a beautiful picket fence around it would never be realized.

Worse than that, he began to run after other women. He even became a drunkard.

ISN'T THERE A BETTER ANSWER?

At this point there arise many questions that demand an answer. Must she remain married to this man? Isn't she entitled to something better than this? Is her entire life to be enslaved to this man who has turned out to be so miserable in so many ways?

The Bible's answer comes back clear and strong: "What God

has joined together, let not man put asunder." The Bible insists that she has been :fused into one flesh with this man. He is her husband. He is not just any man. He is her husband. His life is her life and her life is his life. She is to live out her life in quiet submission to him. True, she is to skillfully and lovingly encourage him. She is to try to help him see his potentials. But she cannot nag him. She cannot boss him. She cannot threaten him. The ideas of separation or divorce must never even enter her thoughts.

Again we are reminded of the old marriage form:

I, Jane, take thee, John, to be my wedded husband, to have and to hold from this day forward, for better for worse, for richer for poorer, in sickness and in health, to love and to cherish, till death do us part according to God's holy ordinance; and thereto I give thee my troth.

The violation in thought of this basic principle that marriage cannot be broken is the major root of so many divorces today. As long as a husband or a wife thinks in his or her mind, "I will love you as long as you are worthy of my love," the disaster of divorce hovers over that marriage. It is the husband's responsibility to love his wife without reservation. And it is the wife's responsibility to love her husband without reservation. Oh, if only husbands and wives could realize the importance of this principle. The husband must make it his business to love his wife, wanting the very best for her. The wife must make it her business to lovingly live in quiet submission to her husband. Each must accept the other totally and fully as part of their life as long as they live.

As illogical, as irrational, as foolish as these principles may appear to the secular mind, they nevertheless are the principles laid down by God Himself. If we disobey them, it is to our own hurt. If we obey them as a child of God, we can know that we have God's blessings, and that is everything!

THE PROBLEM OF CHILDREN

In regards to the marriage bed another point should be made that can be very helpful. It relates to the changes that develop when children are born into the family.

When two people become married, there is a wonderful joy that is experienced by both the husband and the wife. Often, the husband relates most intensively to this because he feels that he is "number one." The wife, in her love for her husband, gladly bestows her attention and her affection on him. He in turn responds by showing great consideration and affection for his wife.

Of course, the beginning of a marriage will not be without problems. The wife at times will have great difficulty in submitting her will to that of her husband. The transition from being a single, independent person to being bound to a husband requires great adjustments in any woman's life. But nevertheless, she has her husband and she wants to be the very best wife.

Likewise, the husband at times may feel burdened by the new responsibilities of having a wife. He, too, has left the freedoms of the single state. Now he feels fettered to his wife. He knows he should always care for her and always want the best for her. But consciously or unconsciously, he may still have moments when he wishes he did not have the responsibility of a wife. And so there will be times of misunderstanding and even of quarreling. But still, they have each other, and each one is still number one in the eyes of the other.

But then the first baby comes. The husband is so proud. Just think! He is the father. And the wife is radiant with the joy of becoming a mother.

But along with this beautiful baby comes another problem. The wife is "oh, so happy" in her motherhood. But a great amount of her time, energy, and affection must be given to this precious infant. And she feels tremendously fulfilled as she showers her love and affection on her baby.

The husband, too, loves his new baby. But soon, he begins to realize he is no longer number one. This new baby has become number one in his wife's love and affection.

If he is mature in his responsibilities, he will understand that there is much more to marriage than just having a loving, submissive wife. One of the most important aspects of marriage is the bringing forth of children. It is God's method of continuing the human race so that God's purposes can be worked out on this earth. In other words, two people who marry each other should understand that a major obligation of marriage is the matter of children.

True, by using birth control devices married couples can avoid or delay the responsiblity of children. But the sinful practice of birth control is not the subject of this study. Presently we are concerned primarily with the fact that a difficult problem can arise when the babies come.

If the husband is immature in this matter (and most husbands are, to some degree), this problem can have devastating results in the marriage. He no longer is the center of his wife's attention. While his wife still loves him and submits herself to his attentions, it seems that she always has the baby on her mind. A competitor is in the house, competing for his wife's affections. And she is gladly sharing her affections with this little competitor.

And then the second baby comes. Now the wife's attention is even further diverted from her husband. The demands of caring for the children, in addition to all of the other domestic responsibilities, leave little energy and concern for the marriage bed.

Now the husband feels more left out than ever. His manhood is being terribly threatened. His wife seems to have become much less responsive to his needs. It seems there is nothing he can do about it.

Wonderfully, in many marriages the husband recognizes his own selfishness and realizes that he must focus his eyes upon his own responsibilities as a parent rather than on his selfish desires with his wife. And in these cases the family ties are actually strengthened by the arrival of children.

But unfortunately, in some marriages the husband does not see his selfishness. All he knows is that he has a wife who does not submit to him the way she did when they were first married. He, therefore, begins to withdraw from his wife. He begins to spurn the intimacies of the marriage bed.

Because his wife is so busy loving and caring for the children, she does not always sense the change in her husband. In fact, she may even think that he has grown somewhat tired of the marriage bed and that he actually welcomes the extended periods during which there is little intimacy. She fails to realize that her husband's pride is being severely damaged. He is withdrawing because he cannot stand the frustration of having a wife whom he believes is not entirely submissive to him.

The outcome of this situation is frequently one of alienation between the husband and the wife. The husband may spend long hours away from the home when he has no compelling reason to be away. He may concentrate his attention on his business, or his hobbies, or his friends. Perhaps the time even comes when separate bedrooms become a way of life for these unhappy parents.

In our day the prevalence of divorce suggests that divorce will be only a little way down the road for such a couple. The wife, who loves her children and her husband, does not understand that her child of a husband feels that he must always be number one in his wife's affections. She does not realize that with the coming of children she needs to demonstrate in a special way that her love and submission to her husband will always come first in her life.

True, if a wife sees her husband pouting or acting selfishly, there is a tremendous temptation on her part to feel offended and to withdraw from her husband. But this kind of action often only intensifies the problem. Instead of just one person acting sinfully in the marriage relationship, now both are acting sinfully. And sin is always destructive. Its outcome is always negative and detrimental to those involved.

It must be noted, of course, that the husband is no less responsible to maintain the marriage relationship in a God-glorifying way than is the wife. Because he is the head of the home, he has an even greater responsibility than the wife. Therefore, when he reacts jealously and selfishly to his wife's affection for their children, his sin is very great. He stands altogether guilty before God.

Wonderfully, many husbands sense their responsibility toward their families. Those families are therefore blessed in many ways.

But what can a wife do who finds that her husband is clearly not as close to her as he was during the early days of their marriage? If she can begin to understand the stress that the coming of the children has placed on her immature husband, she can go a long way in correcting the problem.

Because God has ordained that the husband and wife are to live together in the greatest possible intimacy, the wife who discovers that her husband is beginning to withdraw from that special intimacy should be greatly concerned. While her husband may never admit his frustration or his hurt pride, the wife should nevertheless make sure that her attention to her children and to her domestic duties does not help develop this withdrawal in her child husband.

Because the wife finds great fulfillment as a mother, the intimacies of the marriage bed are usually not as needful in her life as they are in the life of her husband. Therefore, she must be especially alert to withdrawal signs in her husband. Such action on the part of the husband can signal that very difficult times are coming for their marriage.

The wife, therefore, must realize that it is very important for her child husband to be number one in the marriage relationsip. Prayerfully, patiently, tenderly, consistently she should convey to her husband her faithful love for him. Little gestures, loving looks, a touch, all the things that were so important during courtship and the honeymoon should remain in evidence.

If the estrangement has greatly advanced, it may take much time before the husband will sense again the love and devotion his wife has for him. Moreover, because his ardor has become like ice, the wife will need much of God's grace to persistently continue in her efforts to rekindle desire in his heart.

But we can do all things through Christ who strengthens us. To show her love to her husband is entirely in agreement with God's Word. Therefore, as God strengthens her, she is to continue her efforts to show her love to him in every way possible.

Thus far, our study has shown us the immense responsibility that marriage is. We should now look briefly at the matter of courtship as preparation for marriage. This we will do in our next chapter.

CHAPTER 9

COURTSHIP

We have looked at a few of the problems that may occur in the marriage relationship, seeing some of the enormous difficulties a husband and a wife may face in their marriage. It should be obvious that if both spouses are truly saved, the tensions of marriage will be greatly diminished. Even in the case of unsaved couples, God in His mercy frequently restrains sin to the degree that they can live together in relative happiness and contentment.

But in this study we have been looking at the marriage where the tensions have developed to the point that divorce is looming on the horizon. When this situation occurs the unsaved couple has little to help them. Their parents' desires, peer pressure from friends, or a feeling of responsibility toward their children may help keep the marriage going for a while, but because neither spouse recognizes the authority of the Bible, and because their world increasingly condones divorce, the reasonable expectation for this marriage is, unfortunately, divorce.

On the other hand, if one of the spouses is truly a child of God, the expectation for this marriage is much brighter. By God's grace, if the husband is saved, he can do much to protect the continuation of the marriage. By following God's rules he can do much to protect the integrity of his marriage.

Likewise, if the wife is a true child of God, she can be very effective in maintaining the continuation of her marriage.

Of course, the task facing the saved spouse of an unsaved partner who is exceedingly disagreeable to live with is indeed formidable. No individual in their own strength can face some of the difficulties that can arise. Only God's grace can sustain them through very stressful situations.

But God's grace is sufficient. God has given very beautiful and certain promises that can be depended upon entirely. God has promised He will never leave us nor forsake us. God has committed Himself to the principle that all things work together for good for those who love Him (cf. Romans 8:28).

The believer has the assurance that he can bring all his anxieties to his heavenly Father and receive the peace that passes understanding. He knows that God is able to change the situation overnight. He is quite aware that the difficulties being faced are a part of God's plan for his life.

In fact, the believing spouse will discover that the continuing problems arising from being married to an unsaved spouse only cause the believer to trust God more and more. He will not have the wisdom or the strength in himself to continue in the face of the seemingly mountainous difficulties being faced, but how wonderful to know that all of the problems and frustrations can be poured out in prayer to a God who dearly loves His child. With secure knowledge that God in heaven is still in charge, this child of God can face tomorrow.

One of the wonders of God's grace that will grow increasingly clear to the believing spouse is the fact that this earthly life is not "the big picture." We are here for only a few short years. Our time here is like a drop in the ocean compared with the eternity we will spend in the New Heaven and New Earth. Therefore, whatever the trauma that must be faced, it will have an end. And following that welcome end is a life in which there is no suffering nor sorrow nor unhappiness ever again.

Moreover, the saved spouse needs to be keenly aware that the unsaved spouse is on the way to hell. While he may appear to be "getting away" with his selfishness, this is not so at all. The unsaved spouse is to be pitied to the highest possible degree. If he dies without becoming saved, every one of his sins must be paid for. And the payment God demands is eternal damnation.

On the other hand, even though the saved spouse may suffer greatly, the spiritual blessings already enjoyed, along with the certainty of eternity with our Lord, emphasize the fact that the saved spouse has everything on his side.

TAKE CARE WHO YOU DATE

But what steps can be taken to insure a biblical marriage in the first place? The potential awfulness of a marriage between a believer and an unbeliever is so great that a word of caution must be directed to those who are thinking about marriage.

How careful must a person be who is unmarried and who is becoming romantically inclined toward someone? The answer is that he must be exceedingly careful. As we have learned, when two people have become married, the wife is bound to the husband as long as they live. The words "separation" and "divorce" should never be a part of their vocabulary.

Therefore, it is of absolute importance that each knows as much about the other as possible before marriage. Dating and engagement, as we know them in our land, are designed to provide time to acquire this knowledge.

Obviously, if a person discovers that the other person is divorced and their spouse is still living, then it is very foolish to date that person. Even if the divorced person has become a beautiful child of God, marriage should not take place. Even if the divorce took place before this person became saved, there cannot be remarriage. Therefore, it would be exceedingly reckless to date such a person. It would be only to place a huge temptation before both persons.

Likewise, when two people become romantically interested in each other, it is imperative that they pay careful attention to the spiritual condition of the potential partner. How awful it would be if one person only seemed to be saved and after the honeymoon was over the saved spouse discovered that their mate was unsaved.

If on the first few dates the saved person does not find any substantial evidence that the other person is a child of God, then dating should cease. Romantic love has a way of blinding people more than they are willing to admit. Because an unsaved person, who seems to be interested in the things Christian people are interested in, can still have very many attractive qualities, it is very easy to focus only on attractive qualities.

Many a wife who has discovered after the wedding that she was married to an unsaved husband had not been careful enough when she dated. She may have realized at first that all was not spiritually well with this handsome man she was dating, but as she became increasingly attracted to him, she began to rationalize about what he could eventually become.

Surely, he does show a lot of interest in church, she reasons. Surely, her influence is so great in his life that even if he is not already saved, as she witnesses to him and prays for him, he will eventually become saved. Meanwhile, she is becoming more and more blinded by her romantic love.

She has already violated two very important rules. First, dating, engagement, and marriage are not missionary endeavors. If she wants to minister to the unsaved, there are thousands of people all around her who need her witness. But the arena of romance is not the place for missionary work. It is designed to provide, by God's grace, a godly marriage. This must remain the single focus of the dating agreement.

True, there are some instances wherein a child of God has had the glad experience of seeing their steady date become saved. But these unusual exceptions provide no sound basis for this kind of exception. Too many emotions are involved in romantic love. Unless there is clear, immediate and continuing evidence that the one being dated is already a child of God, the only wise action is to cease dating. The reason for this is quite evident.

Suppose at the inception of dating there is good evidence that one person is not a child of God. But the dates continue because many attractive qualities can be seen in the one being dated. The Christian knows the importance of salvation and so encourages the unsaved person to read the Bible, to pray, and to attend church. Because the unsaved person is falling in love with the saved person, he increasingly tries to please her. She, as the saved person, will become more and more convinced that God's Spirit is working in the heart of her steady date. After all, why else is he beginning to attend church so faithfully? Why does he appear to have become so interested in the Bible?

True, at times he says or does things that are quite alien to a saved person. But because she is falling in love with him, she overlooks her fears, trying to see only God's grace in his life. Even when parents and friends express concern, she will not listen. Because she has fallen in love, she has convinced herself that God's grace is present in his life. Moreover, she is sure that after they are married he will grow even faster in the things of the Lord.

So they marry each other. Now he has her as his wife. By the time the honeymoon is over he knows he does not have to try as hard to please her. Because going to church and studying the Bible are boring to him, he will soon cease doing these things altogether.

The happy bride eventually discovers to her utter consternation that she is married to an unsaved husband. She realizes, too, that she is married to him until death parts them.

But because her husband does not recognize God's rules against divorce, there is a strong likelihood that when he gets tired of living with a wife who puts such a high premium on going to church and reading the Bible, he will seek a divorce. This may even come when the family has grown to include children.

And so the believing wife becomes divorced. According to the Bible, she may never marry again as long as her husband is living. But in his rebellion against God he marries someone else, and she is left with the heavy responsibility of rearing the children.

Unfortunately this sad scenario is being repeated again and again in our day in actual life situations. If only those who are free to marry would realize the enormous consequences of marriage! One can never be too careful in deciding who to date.

Some may argue that dating is quite innocent, and that it does not necessarily have to be pointing to marriage. But the fact is that all dating, however innocuous, superficial and innocent it may appear to be, is a preliminary step toward marriage. Ordinarily, every marriage begins with a first date. It is a ritual that is engaged in to prepare for a successful marriage.

Therefore, during courtship the chief focus should be on

spiritual concerns. Serious questions should be faced such as: What is salvation? What does it mean to be born again? What is the true Gospel? If we should marry, what church would we attend? If God gave us children, what about baptism? What about the education of those children? What kind of school would we try to send them to? What is the wife's chief role in marriage? Is she to be first an assistant breadwinner and then a keeper of the home? Or is she first to be a keeper of the home and assist as a breadwinner only if it does not interfere with her duties at home? What about family devotions? What about the responsibility of giving to God's work? What about the use of birth control measures? Etc., etc.

All such questions should be faced and settled before marriage. By facing these questions, at least two goals will be realized. First of all, it will provide a forum for the examination of the spiritual sensitivities of each person. Two people may each be convinced the other person is a child of God, but if agreement cannot be realized on these issues, it may raise serious doubts as to the advisability of marriage. These are all matters of serious concern in the life of a true child of God. Therefore, to enter into the intimate, binding relationship of marriage with basic disagreements on these issues may be exceedingly dangerous. If the two disagree on these issues during courtship, the disagreements are sure to intensify during marriage.

On the other hand, by honestly and openly facing these issues before marriage, a solid foundation can be laid for a happy, God-glorifying marriage. If there is honest agreement on these matters, both will enter into marriage secure in the knowledge that harmony will prevail.

Hopefully we have come to an understanding of what is likely to bring about a more perfect marriage union.

But what about those who divorced before they were saved? Are they free to remarry? What about those who are already married a second or third time? Are they to divorce their wives in order to become more biblical? We will look at these questions in our next and final chapter.

CHAPTER 10

SOME FINAL QUESTIONS

We have spent considerable time investigating the biblical principles that relate to the binding nature of the marriage union. Repeatedly, we found that there is not to be divorce under any circumstances whatsoever. What God has joined together is not to be put asunder. Moreover, if someone does become divorced for some reason, we found that it would be a grievous sin to remarry while the former spouse still lives.

We then looked briefly at the implications of these truths upon both the husband's role and the wife's role in the marriage relationship. We discovered that, even if both spouses are saved, it can be very difficult to be the kind of husband and wife that God desires. But when one spouse is unsaved, it is certain that the other will have an exceedingly difficult life to live.

However, by God's grace it is possible to live victoriously even in such a difficult marriage. But to do so requires very careful obedience to God's rules. Wonderfully, God has given us His rules and principles so that even in the most trying circumstances we can experience the blessings of obedience. Those blessings include not only the comforting knowledge that we are living in the will of God, but they sometimes include the salvation of the unsaved spouse as well.

But now we will look at some other questions that often arise in Christian circles. For example, isn't it true that when we become a Christian old things have passed away and all things have become new? Doesn't this imply that if I was divorced before I was saved, now that I am saved I, as a new creature, am free to remarry? And what am I to do if I become saved after I have already married a second time? Let's conclude our study by examining such questions.

DIVORCE AND THE NEWLY SAVED

A common assertion these days is the idea that if we were divorced before we were saved, after becoming saved we are free to remarry. This is based on the contention that as saved people we have become new creatures in Christ. Old things have passed away and all things have become new. But is this kind of teaching biblical?

Actually, this teaching is quite unbiblical. First, it does not recognize that God's laws apply to all mankind. For example, the commandments "thou shalt not kill" or "thou shalt not covet" apply to the unbeliever as well as to the believer. The only difference is in the response to these commands. The true believer earnestly desires to be obedient to all of God's commands, while the unbeliever pays little or no attention to these rules.

The true believer knows that all of the commands of the Bible are to be obeyed. There is no statement of the Bible he would disregard. Therefore, if the Bible says he is not to remarry after divorce, then he will remain single. And this is true whether he was divorced before or after he was saved.

Secondly, becoming a new creature in Christ does not necessarily nullify the physical results of our sin. For example, a murderer is sentenced to the electric chair. While waiting to be executed, he becomes saved. This means he will never be threatened with hell for murder or for any other sin he committed. He now stands absolutely blameless before God. But does this mean that now he can leave death row and avoid execution? No, he still must be executed for his crime, unless he receives a very unusual pardon from the governor.

The same is true of a drunkard. Because of his continued drunkenness he is told he is dying of liver disease. But then he becomes saved. All of his sins, including drunkenness, have been covered by Christ's blood. But does this also mean that he will not die of liver disease? Not necessarily. Normally, the effects of his drunkenness continue with him.

Likewise, the man who has a messed up life because of divorce can be forgiven of this sin along with every other sin he has ever committed. When he becomes saved he can know that he will never have to answer to God for any of these sins.

But much of the impact of those sins remains with him. God's laws concerning marriage and divorce still stand. Even if he becomes saved after he was divorced, he knows that God's law prohibits remarriage while his former spouse is living. Therefore, he will remain single as God has commanded.

This leads us into another question. Is it really true that God expects those who were divorced to live the single life in total celibacy? Isn't that asking too much? Surely a loving, forgiving heavenly Father would not expect this.

These questions can be answered from two vantage points. First of all, let us look at a marriage that was broken by God. Consider the example of a widow with five children, one of whom is a child with special needs. God has taken her husband by death.

Biblically she is free to remarry, and if any family needs a husband and a father, it is certainly this one. But in actuality, marriage for this widow is highly unlikely. It would be difficult enough to expect a new husband to become the instantaneous father of five children. But it is well nigh impossible for a new husband to be willing to take on the additional responsibilities of a child with special needs and cares.

Now, did God leave this poor widow in an impossible, terrible situation? Surely God is perfect in His actions and His wisdom! Therefore, when God took this husband by death God knew full well that the widow could continue a meaningful and happy life without the presence of a husband and father for her children.

True, it would be a life that would be different from what the world considers to be ideal. She would certainly need the help of others. And she would have to constantly cry out to God for wisdom and patience. But she would find that God's grace is truly sufficient. In fact, she could experience in an especially dynamic way the reality of such promises as "I will never leave thee, nor forsake thee" (Hebrews 13:5).

So, if God's grace is sufficient for those whose marriages have been broken by His own action, surely we can expect that His grace will be sufficient for those whose marriages have been tampered with by man's action of divorce.

There is a second emphasis here that must be kept in mind. In our sinful, finite mind we think that because the intimacies enjoyed in our marriage were such a seemingly necessary part of our life, that it would be nearly impossible to live a celibate life after divorce. "How can I be expected to live the rest of my life without any further intimacies with the opposite sex? Surely a good God does not intend that for me," we reason.

But God is the one who has designed us. It is God Himself who has put the body chemistry within us so that we can enjoy the intimacies of marriage.

It is also God who assures us that it is possible for humans to live very happy lives without the benefit of such intimacies. God declares in I Corinthians 7:27,..."Art thou loosed from a wife? seek not a wife." He adds in verses 32-34:

But I would have you without carefulness. He that is unmarried careth for the things that belong to the Lord, how he may please the Lord:

But he that is married careth for the things that are of the world, how he may please his wife.

There is difference also between a wife and a virgin. The unmarried woman careth for the things of the Lord, that she may be holy both in body and in spirit: but she that is married careth for the things of the world, how she may please her husband.

These verses clearly show that there are some special advantages that are available to the unmarried. In these verses God is not speaking to a certain group within the company of the believers. He is speaking to all who have become children of God.

Jesus spoke to this question in Matthew 19:12 where He taught:

For there are some eunuchs, which were so born from their mother's womb: and there are some eunuchs, which were made eunuchs of men: and there be eunuchs, which have made themselves eunuchs for the kingdom of heaven's sake. He that is able to receive it, let him receive it.

The strict definition of a eunuch is someone who is not physically equipped to perform the sexual act. But Jesus is teaching that some people make themselves eunuchs for the sake of the kingdom of heaven. But He is not implying that they are to have themselves physically altered. Rather, they choose to live without the physical intimacy of the marriage relationship. In denying themselves this intimacy, they gain all kinds of new and wonderful ways to live to God's glory.

True, the world in which we live has put an enormous priority on sexual intimacy. Listening to the advertisements, the novels, the TV programs, the psychologists of our day, we have been brainwashed into thinking that if we cannot have this kind of intimacy, we are being deprived of the greatest blessing known to man.

But this is a lie. God's Word is the truth. While God indicates there are certain blessings within the marriage relationship -- particularly in the rearing of godly children -- there are even greater blessings to be realized in the single state. This is what we learn from I Corinthians 7:32-34.

The single person has the advantage of having more time to serve the Lord by doing such good works as caring for the lonely, the children of broken homes, and the elderly in nursing homes. They also have more time for Bible study and prayer.

Married people should also be involved in denying themselves so that their lives might be as fruitful as possible for Christ. But it is in the lives of the unmarried that these ideals can be realized to the highest degree.

And it is this spiritual dimension that can make the big difference in the lives of widows, widowers, divorced people, and those who have never married. God has given this special comfort and promise to all those who are single.

But it is only as they live in accordance with God's principles that these added blessings become evident. If the single person listens to the advice of the world, the feeling that the single state makes a person a deprived, pitiable, second-class citizen can be overwhelming. This in turn can set the stage for a fall into fornication. Only when God's rules are followed can the life of the single person become even more victorious than that of the married person.

But now we should face another question. What about someone who has married a second or even a third time and then become saved? Is he or she to divorce these latter spouses? What is to be done in order to obey God?

THE SECOND MARRIAGE

The question we are facing is a serious one, even though it should not be. If the human race, led by the church, were obeying God's laws concerning marriage and divorce, there would be very few second marriages. But because of the wholesale repudiation of God's laws concerning the sanctity of marriage, this problem has become enormous. Everywhere we turn we meet those who have remarried after divorce. Therefore, we must try to find an answer to this question.

We already know that the second marriage is an adulterous marriage. Remember, the wife is bound to the husband as long as he lives. And Romans 7:3 plainly declares:

So then if, while her husband liveth, she be married to another man, she shall be called an adulteress: but if her husband be dead, she is free from that law; so that she is no adulteress, though she be married to another man.

We cannot deny the clear teaching set forth in this verse. The wife is an adulteress if she is married to a second husband while her first husband is still living. She is an adulteress because her first marriage has become adulterated by her divorce, as well as because she has married a second husband.

We must recognize that a number of examples are given in the Bible of men with multiple wives. Jacob had four wives, David had several wives, and Solomon had 700 wives and 300 concubines! But, these were exceptions. The usual example that is given is of one wife. This was true of Adam, Noah, Isaac, Moses, etc.

We also consider that never did the Bible instruct a man to divorce all but the first wife. This is remarkable when we remember that the principle of one man, one wife goes all the way back to the beginning. God did not tell Adam that the three or four or several shall become one flesh. No. He instructed mankind in the beginning that the two shall be one flesh (Genesis 2:24). Although in Genesis 2:24 the number "two" is not used, the verse speaks of a man cleaving to his wife (not wives) "and they shall be one flesh."

Therefore shall a man leave his father and his mother, and shall cleave unto his wife: and they shall be one flesh.

Remember, Jesus quotes this verse in Matthew 19:5 and Mark 10:8. In both of these verses He declares that the two shall be one flesh.

Therefore, we might expect that God would ask those who have violated this command by taking multiple wives to divorce their additional wives. But such an admonition is not given by God.

Thus, we must realize that even though God has willed that the proper marriage is one husband, one wife, nevertheless He has allowed mankind to break this law by having multiple wives. Nowhere in the Bible does He ask those believers with multiple wives to divorce the extra wives.

The reason for this state of affairs probably lies in the fact that even the marriage of a second wife is still a marriage. Even though it is altogether wrong, for some reason God still counts it as a marriage. Thus, the second wife becomes bound to the husband even as the first wife has become bound to the husband. And once this binding relationship occurs, there cannot be a breaking of that relationship.

True, the marriage to the second wife adulterates the pristine, ideal character of marriage as a one husband, one wife relationship. But the second marriage still is a marriage, and therefore, there can be no divorce.

When a man divorces his first wife, she is still bound to him from God's vantage point. Therefore, when he takes a second wife while his first wife is living, he has two wives bound to him. The act of divorcing his first wife was grievous sin. Likewise, the act of marrying a second wife was grievous sin. But the second marriage was still a marriage, and therefore, there cannot be divorce from this second wife. This is the marriage in which he must continue until death separates him from this wife.

True, a second or third marriage under these circumstances is far from ideal. From the standpoint of its relationship to the first marriage, it is adulterous. Secondly, there still exist responsibilities towards the first wife. Alimony and child support are the most obvious. But there are also moral and spiritual responsiblities and conflicts that may continue to plague the one who has arrogantly violated God's rules. Unfortunately, the children frequently suffer the most because of these selfish parents.

Moreover, such a husband can no longer be a pastor, an elder, or a deacon within the church. In I Timothy 3 God specifically instructs that such an office bearer in the church is to be the husband of one wife. Remember that in Romans 7:3 God speaks of the woman's husband still living while she is married to another man. God considers her to have two husbands, even though she is legally divorced from the first. Likewise, from God's vantage point, the man who has divorced his first wife and married another now has two wives. Therefore, he does not meet God's qualifications for a pastor, an elder, or a deacon.

In spite of the difficulties of a second marriage after divorce, it is still a marriage. The spouses involved are to live as if it were their first marriage.

Wonderfully, if they have become true believers, they can know that all of the sins connected with the divorce and remarriage are covered by Christ's blood. Christ came for sinners, not righteous people. Regardless of how many dirty, rotten sins we may have committed, when Jesus becomes our Savior we can know that He has paid for all our sins.

This brings us to the last group of questions we shall consider in this study. If a second marriage is to be lived the same as a first marriage with the complete assurance that the sins of divorce and remarriage become completely forgiven by God, why can't I just go ahead into a second marriage and then ask God's forgiveness later? Suppose I am already married to someone, but I want to marry someone else with whom I have fallen in love. Why can't I go ahead and get an unbiblical divorce and then sinfully marry this second person? Cannot I then ask God's forgiveness, believing Christ's blood will cover these sins? Or, suppose I am divorced; can't I first marry someone else before I get right with God? That way I can have my second marriage and Christ also. Then I don't have to live the rest of my natural life in the single state.

These questions and observations surely seem logical and attractive. They surely appear to solve the problem of one having his cake and eating it too.

But this course of action is fraught with danger. Effectively, the one contemplating this action is taking the role of an adversary of Almighty God. Effectively he is saying, "I can sin as deeply and as often as I wish, and in my own sweet time I can become saved. And God must save me when I am ready to become saved."

Such a one is tempting God like Israel tested God in the wilderness when they complained that God was leading them to destruction. God warns in I Corinthians 10:9:

Neither let us tempt Christ, as some of them also tempted, and were destroyed of serpents.

The specific sin God had in view in this verse is recorded in Numbers 21:5-6 where we read:

And the people spake against God, and against Moses, Wherefore have ye brought us up out of Egypt to die in the wilderness? for there is no bread, neither is there any water; and our soul loatheth this light bread.

And the Lord sent fiery serpents among the people, and they bit the people; and much people of Israel died.

The nation of Israel accused God of being too harsh in bringing them out of Egypt into the wilderness where they were to live following God's direction. But their complaints against God only brought judgment upon them.

So, too, those who insist on having their own way concerning divorce or remarriage after divorce effectively are complaining that God's way is too severe and too harsh. They are insisting on having their own way.

Ancient Israel insisted on having its own way and as a result came under God's wrath. How then can we expect God to treat any differently those who insist on having their own way in such important matters as divorce and remarriage? Indeed, it is a very serious matter to contend with Almighty God!

Moreover, the idea that I can sin for as long as I like, then sometime in the future I can repent at will and secure God's grace, is entirely faulty. It does not recognize nor understand the nature of God's grace.

We must remember that mankind is not the decision maker in salvation. Only Sovereign God Himself decides who is to be saved. But He comes to us commanding us to believe in Christ as Savior. He warns, "How shall we escape, if we neglect so great salvation" (Hebrews 2:3)? He exhorts,..."make your calling and election sure...." (I Peter 1:10). And He instructs us that we are to come not despise" (Psalms 51:17). He also warns that He resists the proud and gives grace to the humble.

With such warnings and exhortations before our eyes how would anyone dare to deliberately rebel against God in something as serious as divorce or remarriage after divorce?

These are not sins that one slips into incidentally or accidentally. These are sins that require deliberate planning and consistent action over a period of considerable time. And if one's heart is rebellious and hard enough today to commit such a sin, the probability is that this person is not saved. Moreover, it is evidence that God is not even drawing this one toward salvation. If God is today allowing this person to engage in such rebellion, what assurance can he have that later on God will deal kindly with him and soften his heart in order to draw him to salvation?

We may never presume upon the mercies of God. Today is the day of salvation. No person has any guarantee or promise that he will even be alive tomorrow. How then can we know that tomorrow we can be able to make our peace with God?

Furthermore, if we are so rebellious today that we would dare to sin so deliberately, how do we know that at some future date our hearts will become broken before God so that we can honestly and sincerely cry out for mercy? Indeed, we have no such assurance.

Therefore, to deliberately divorce or remarry after divorce, knowing that such action is contrary to God's will, is the most foolish and dangerous action anyone could take. The only fulfilling way to live is in accordance with God's laws. And the best time to begin living in this way is right now. May God give wisdom to those who have even played with the idea of sinning now and repenting later!

HOW DID IT HAPPEN

But now let's turn our thoughts to wondering how it could ever have happened that the dreadful sin of divorce has become so widespread in our day.

The problem of unbiblical marriage and divorce is so serious, so catastrophic, that we wonder how the church could ever have strayed so far from the truth. Fifty years ago it was only in the more rebellious elements of the secular world that this sin was visible. Because the church would not even countenance this sin, the secular world did not dare to go too deeply into sin. It is a fact that the church is to some degree the conscience of the secular world.

But then comes along a dear lady who was married to a man living adulterously with other women. The church began to wonder: "Must this dear wife continue to live with that kind of horrible husband?" So in its sympathy and compassion, the church restudied the question of divorce for adultery and finally decided, "Yes, the Bible does allow divorce for adultery." And so the door was opened so that not only could this dear lady have her divorce, but also many others in the congregation could begin to lawfully seek divorce. Because the church is to some degree the conscience of the secular world, the people of the world also began to expand their divorce horizons. And so divorce began to multiply in the world.

At this point another kind of problem began to arise. Another dear lady was deserted by her husband and she had to labor all alone in caring for her children. But there was a dear Christian man who loved her and wanted to marry her. Surely, they reasoned, it must be in accordance with God's will for those children to have a Christian father to care for them!

So again the church, in its pity and compassion for this woman, appointed study committees to research the possibilities of biblical divorce for desertion and biblical remarriage after divorce. And again victory was assured. Indeed, these theologians successfully convinced themselves that the Bible allows divorce for desertion and remarriage after divorce. And so not only could this dear lady divorce her scoundrel of a husband, but she was free to marry this fine Christian man who had fallen in love with her.

Many in the church now believe they have God's blessing to divorce and remarry. Indeed, even deacons and pastors are now freely divorcing and remarrying. And the world, taking its cue from the church, becomes a wasteland of broken homes.

Simultaneously, the church, taking its cue from the world, tacitly gives assent to the dreadful sin of birth control. This not only encourages the world to go deeper into this particular sin, but also opens the door to increased fornication. Where forty years ago it was rightly considered to be shameful and repugnant for unmarried individuals of the opposite sex to live together, now it has become commonplace. Indeed, sexual restraints of any kind have almost disappeared.

Along with all of these step-by-step violations of God's laws for the protection of the family unit, have come shattered lives of men, women, and children whose families have been hopelessly broken. The havoc is so widespread and of such magnitude that no words can accurately describe the full extent of the horror story.

Indeed, it is no wonder that God's judgment is on the church of today. I am afraid that the primary blame for the destruction of the marriage institution and the family unit must be placed at the door of the church, for it has the Word of God that indicates divorce is not to be countenanced. The church is the institution that has rewritten the rules to accommodate these sins of its members.

But what can we do? We must do the same thing that must

always be done when we find sin in our lives. We must repent! We must turn away from all of these rebellious rules that permit divorce and remarriage. We must cry out to God for His mercy and forgiveness.

And we can't wait for another denomination or even an other church within our denomination to agree with us that we have sinned. I personally must repent if I have had wrong thinking about these questions. And the church I belong to must repent.

Unfortunately, few will repent. The sins that have developed and have been accepted as the marriage institution has been slowly but surely destroyed are so widespread and so interwoven into the fabric of our churches that there is little hope for that. This is particularly so because we are so close to the end of the world. These dreadful sins evidence the fulfillment of the prophecy that most men's love will grow cold. May God have mercy on us!

Wonderfully, however, those who truly want to be obedient to God's Word can still move in the direction of a more holy life. If we discover wrong practices or wrong doctrines in our life, we can repent of them. God is gracious. He does forgive! And the Bible is just as much a guide for our lives today as it has ever been.

Could it be that there will be those who humbly will give heed to all that God teaches? Although we cannot turn this massive destruction of the family around, individually we can grow in holiness by becoming more obedient. This is the heart's desire of every child of God.